Parents' Guide For Helping Kids Become "A" Students

by Anne Farrell, Jacqueline Watson,
& Elaine Dundas

Parents, this book is for you. Your involvement in your child's education is the most important contribution you can make to fulfilling his potential as a happy and productive adult.

This book contains practical activities for improving reading, math, spelling, writing, homework, memory, notetaking, and test-taking. A special feature is Family Talk & Read Sessions designed to improve oral communication.

Get involved!

Recent publicity on this book:

Small Press Top 40—September 1990
Saddleback Valley News, CA (Aug 29, 1990)—"A Dianetics for the parents of school children."
Los Angeles Times (Oct 11, 1990)—"Provides parents with specific ideas and strategies on how to help their children succeed in school."

Parents' Guide for Helping
Kids Become "A" Students

Published by:

BLUE BIRD PUBLISHING
1713 East Broadway #306
Tempe AZ 85282
(602) 968-4088
FAX (602) 983-7319
Toll-free credit card orders
1-800-654-1993

ISBN 0-933025-21-1 $11.95

Library of Congress Cataloging-in-Publication Data

Farrell, Anne, 1927-
    Parents' guide for helping kids become "A" Students / Anne
Farrell, Jacqueline Watson, and Elaine Dundas.
        p.   cm.
    Includes index.
    ISBN 0-933025-21-1 : $11.95
        1. Education--United States--Parent participation. 2. Reading-
-United States--Parent participation. 3. Study, Method of.
4. Academic achievement--United States. I. Watson, Jacqueline,
1942- . II. Dundas, Elaine, 1921- . III. Title.
LB1048.5.F37   1990
    649'.68--dc20   90-48413
                                                              CIP

ABOUT THE AUTHORS

Anne Farrell worked as a resource specialist at the junior high level in the Capistrano Unified School District from 1973 until her retirement in 1989. She has a B.A. and an M.A. in history, with elementary and community college credentials and is a licensed resource specialist for the state of California.

Jacqueline Watson has worked as a resource specialist at the elementary level in the Capistrano Unified School District since 1973. She has a B.A. in Elementary Education and is a licensed resource specialist for the state of California.

Elaine Dundas has taught elementary school for several years. She has also taught speech at the high school and college level. She presently teaches a class in effective communication for adults at the San Diego Community College District. Her previous writing credits include two articles on speech for *Specialty Salesman* magazine; poems for children published in *Humpty Dumpty* and *Turtle* magazines; and an article for *San Diego Home Garden Magazine*.

Dedication

From Anne Farrell and Jacqueline Watson:
For all the children who have taught us so much
and to Wayne, Shannon, Randy, and Kathy.

From Elaine Dundas:
To all parents who want to help their children
Be all that they can be.

TABLE OF CONTENTS

INTRODUCTION

Parents, this book is for you. Through our experience as teachers, we have found that you are always interested in ways to help your children in school. Because so many of you have asked for suggestions on how you can help your children, we felt there was a universal desire on the part of parents to have information available to them. We have compiled a book that will give you specific ideas and strategies on how to help your child succeed in school.

Your involvement in your child's school experience is the most vital and important contribution you can make to fulfilling his potential as a happy and productive adult. You and the school should be working partners in a relationship based on educating your child to his fullest potential.

Get involved!

FOREWORDS

For a student to be a winner in school requires much the same as it does for an individual to be successful in any endeavor. This includes ability, interest, hard work, and helpful advice from others. It is only the exceptional student who breezes through school with all A's while putting forth little effort. For most students, the road to success is paced with personal diligence and considerable assistance from teachers and other adults.

Research has shown that students who do well in school have parents who are actively involved in their education. This publication is intended to provide a guide to parents so they can be equipped to work with their children.

Often parents want to help, but they don't know how. Here is a book that tells parents how. The authors, in promoting a collaborative approach between teacher and parent, provide the best opportunity for each student to become a winner, an "A" student.

Jerome R. Thornsley, Ph.D.
District Superintendent
Capistrano Unified School District
San Juan Capistrano, California

This book is a must for parents and students! As an educator, I recognize that successful students receive encouragement and help from their parents. The authors have captured the essence of how to learn in this innovative new book. Study and organizational skills, testing tips, and math and reading skills are presented in a simple, well organized and informative way.

Jean Trygstad
Principal, Niguel Hills Junior High
Laguna Niguel, California

PART ONE

ACTIVITIES FOR

IMPROVED GRADES

Chapter One: Reading Comprehension

CHAPTER ONE
READING COMPREHENSION

The purpose of this chapter is to show parents easy activities to improve how well their children understand what they are reading. More activities for reading and speaking are included in Part Two: Family Talk & Read Sessions. To help children learn to read, use *Dr. Christman's Learn-to-Read Book*, a phonics program for all ages. Order form at the end of this book.

The goal of all reading is comprehension: getting meaning from the written word. It is a continual thinking process. We generally read for a purpose and it involves the knowledge of specific skills. The basic building blocks of written language are:

1. <u>Words</u>. Word meanings are the basis of all reading—and communication in general. Without understanding what the words mean, it is impossible to comprehend reading. For example: "The Romans were a very prosperous people." In this sentence, it is necessary to know what <u>prosperous</u> means. Otherwise, the sentence has no meaning.

2. <u>Phrases</u>. Phrases are meaningful groups of words. This is the next step toward comprehension. Expressions like "toward a gurgling brook" and "in a steep ravine" are units of words that could cause problems if the reader does not know what those phrases mean.

3. <u>Sentences</u>. A sentence is a complete thought. The sentence must be meaningful to the reader in order for him to comprehend the written material. For example:

"The missionary rambled down the crooked creek." The reader must use his knowledge of word meanings, phrases, and sentences in order to fully understand the sentence.

4. Paragraphs. A paragraph is a group of sentences with one basic idea. It helps to know that the parts of a paragraph are the topic sentence, supporting ideas, and the closing statement. Sometimes the basic idea is inferred rather than directly stated, so the reader must pay close attention to the all of the written material in order to catch its meaning.

Suggestions for Improving Reading

✓ You learn to read by reading. Read to your child and with your child. Start reading to your child when he is a toddler. Continue to read with him as often as possible as he is learning to read, and through the elementary grades.

✓ Children learn to appreciate reading if they see that their parents appreciate reading. Be sure there are plenty of books in the house and that the children see you reading often.

✓ Experiences are important for understanding reading. The more experiences a child has, the more he brings to his reading. For example: a visit to the zoo followed by a book about zoo animals makes the reading more exciting.

✓ Reading aloud improves comprehension for the young child.

✓ Read for a purpose. Understanding improves when you are reading for a reason.

✓ Discuss your child's reading with him.

✓ Reread any parts of the story he doesn't understand.

✓ Help your child form mental pictures as he reads.

✓ Read using hand movements. It increases concentration and understanding.

✓ Use a dictionary to look up unknown words.

✓ Reread your child's favorite stories. He'll discover something new each time he hears them!

THREE ACTIVITIES FOR IMPROVED READING

The following activities will give you ideas of how to improve your child's reading skills. The activities will result in your child being a more active reader. A student of any age will benefit from these methods. For more complicated material, the child will need to learn to take notes—see the Notetaking Chapter.

Activity #1. Active Reading

Step 1. You and your child should try to guess what the story will be about from its title.

Step 2. Have your child read the first page aloud to find out what the story is about.

Step 3. After the first page, discuss whether his guess about the story was correct. Have him read any sentences to you the prove his guess was right or wrong.

Step 4. Repeat this for each page. At the beginning of the page, have the child guess what will happen next. Read the page, then discuss whether his guess was right or wrong. You can do this by asking questions such as: "What do you think the story is about now?" or "What do you think will happen next?" "Why?"

Step 5. Ask your child what he though were the four most important words he learned from the story. Discuss them.

Activity #2. Looking for Answers

The second activity involves taking information from the reading and answering questions about it. There are three ways to look for answers in a reading passage:

In The Sentences—

Ask a question about a particular sentence. The answer should be found in that sentence. For example: "Before the race, the eager teammates practiced their rowing techniques." From this sentence, you could ask: "When did the team practice their rowing?" or "What did the teammates practice before the race?" This type of question is usually a rephrasing of the sentence itself.

On This Page—

Ask a question that can be answered from material on a page your child just read. Sometimes the child may need to look in more than one sentence or paragraph to find the answer.

From Your Brain—

Ask a question about the reading material that involves your child using his own experience and knowledge to answer the question.

Activity #3. Unison Reading

This activity is a method in which you and your child read together. It will improve your child's overall reading. It changes a word-by-word reader into a fluent reader. It increases your child's vocabulary through continual exposure to words. When done daily, it can lead to a marked improvement in reading skills and comprehension. If you have just 10 minutes a day to help your child improve his reading, this is the best method for overall success.

The steps to follow are:

1. First choose a book for your child that is easy. Later books can increase in difficulty.

2. You should read aloud along with your child for 10-15 minutes in daily sessions. During the early sessions, you should read slightly louder and faster than your child, but not so fast that he garbles his words or becomes frustrated.

3. Sit on your child's dominant side, usually the side of the hand he writes with. Your voice should be close to his ear.

4. Move your finger under the words as you read. Your child should read along with you in a smooth, continuous fashion. Make sure that you read at a normal reading speed. It is absolutely essential that the finger movements, voice, and words all be simultaneous.

5. At no time do you correct your child or stop to sound out the words. He will hear them correctly from you, so don't worry. Don't ask questions about the material. Instead, concentrate on smooth reading.

6. Pacing is important. The reading rate should be gradually increased. The student is literally dragged to higher rates of speed in the reading process.

Additional Resources for Reading Comprehension

Anderson, R. C., et al. *Becoming a Nation of Readers: The Report of the Commission on Reading*. University of Illinois, 1985.

Birlem, Ellen and Katherine Wisendanger. *Parent: Help Your Child Become a Better Reader*. R & E Publishers, 1982.

Cooperman, Paul. *Taking Books to Heart: How to Develop a Love of Reading in Your Child*. Addison-Wesley, 1986.

D'Angostino, Robert A. *Mastering Reading Comprehension Skills*. Arco Publishing, 1982.

Graves, Ruth, ed. *The RIF Guide to Encouraging Young Readers*. Reading is Fundamental, 1987.

Sobol, Tom & Harriet. *Your Child in School: Kindergarten Through Second Grade*. Arbor House, 1987.

Sobol, Tom & Harriet. *Your Child in School: The Intermediate Years: Grades Three Through Five*. Arbor House, 1987.

Trelease, Jim. *The New Read-Aloud Handbook*. Penguin Books, 1982. Also available on tape.

CHAPTER TWO
SPELLING

This chapter gives easy-to-follow instructions for improving children's spelling. Special study methods are shown that have been successful in teaching spelling.

Spelling research has been going on for years and has given us some basic generalizations which we can use as a guide when we help our children learn their spelling words:

1. <u>Spelling words should be studied in list form</u>. The initial presentation of the words should be in list form. The words can later be studied in sentences.

2. <u>A pretest should be taken at home or school</u>. One of the most important factors in learning a spelling list occurs when the student immediately corrects his own spelling test by pointing to every letter as you spell the word aloud to him. For that reason, a pretest is a good tool for learning spelling.

3. <u>Short daily spelling sessions are best</u>. Research shows that sessions of 15 minutes each are most effective. After this length of time, motivation and attitude decline.

4. <u>Provide the student with a study method</u>. A student needs to establish an easy-to-follow method to learn to study each word. It should incorporate seeing the correct visual spelling of the whole word and hearing the accurate pronunciation of each word.

5. <u>Motivation is the key to spelling success</u>. Always be sure your child experiences

some success each week on his spelling test in order for him not to become frustrated and disillusioned. If he is not experiencing some success, see your child's teacher about having him take fewer words per week or having easier spelling words until he catches on.

6. <u>Reward your child each week</u>. A reward will motivate your child to study harder. A trip to McDonald's® at the end of the week is more motivating than an "A" on his report card 6 or 8 weeks away!

Study Method for Each Word

Rule #4 above says to provide a study method. This following is a systematic method fo studying spelling words. It used daily, it should help your child learn his spelling words. If he does not experience success with this particular procedure, other methods are provided later in this chapter. Keep trying until you find the method best suited to your child.

1. Put the word to be learned on a 3 x 5 index card. Look at the word and say it with your child.

2. Have your child trace each letter with his index finger.

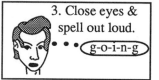

3. It may help your child to see the word by writing the letters in the air with his fingers as he spells it. If he makes an error, go back to step #1.

4. Check to see
if you were right.

(going)

4. The child should look at the word and check each letter to see if he spelled it correctly.

5. Write
the word.

going

5. Cover the word and have the child write it from memory.

6. Look at word
to see if you
wrote it correctly.

6. Have the child look at the word again to see if he wrote it correctly.

A Spelling Schedule

Day 1: Give a pretest on the word list. Pick any five words missed and used the suggested study method for these words.

Day 2: Go over Day 1 words and add five more to study.

Day 3: Review the previous ten words and add five new ones.

Day 4: Review and learn all words left. Your child should now be ready for his spelling test.

Points to Remember:

☞Stick to the schedule.

☞Put the list in a safe place. A lost list is no help!

☞Study only 15 minutes a night.

☞Repeat any of the steps in the procedure as needed to learn the word.

Additional Hints to Improve Spelling

      While the student should approach the study of word lists using the previously described study method, certain hints will help the student remember the words better.

Hint #1. Syllabication (Say the parts of the word)

      For learning longer words, the child will need to break apart the word and say each part, or syllable, as it is written. Sometimes he will be distorting the sound of the syllable in order to remember how the word is spelled. What is is really doing with this technique is saying the word as it is <u>writ-ten</u>, not as it is <u>said</u>. Example: pronounce Wednesday as Wed—nes—day.

Hint #2. Pronunciation (Say the word clearly)

      Mispronunciation accounts for many spelling errors. Speaking is not the same as writing. Words are distorted as we speak so we need to say our words distinctly. For example, "gimme" is not the same as "give me." Be sure the child is given the correct pronunciation of the words, and insist that he enunciate clearly.

Hint #3. Acronym Link (Silly sentences)

      Help the child invent a sentence based on each letter of the spelling word. Example: <u>arithmetic</u>: **A** <u>r</u>at <u>i</u>n <u>t</u>he <u>h</u>ouse <u>m</u>ight <u>e</u>at <u>t</u>he <u>i</u>ce <u>c</u>ream.

Hint #4. Definitional Link (The meaning of the word)

      The meaning of the word can sometimes provide a clue to the correct spelling. Example: A b<u>ee</u>ch is a tr<u>ee</u>. (each has <u>ee</u>)

            A b<u>ea</u>ch is land by the s<u>ea</u>. (each has <u>ea</u>)

Hint #5. Built-In Word (Small word inside a bigger word)

      Create a sentence that links a smaller words to a larger word. Example: You h<u>ear</u> with your <u>ear</u>.

Hint #6. Electronic Speller

A valuable tool your child may find helpful is an electronic speller. When you type in a word spelled phonetically, it scans the word and then gives you the correct spelling. There are many good ones on the market. They are compact and about the size of a pocket calculator.

ADDITIONAL STUDY METHODS FOR SPELLING

The 6-step method for studying each spelling word that has already been described has been found to be the most effective way to learn new words, but some students succeed with other methods. These are included so that you can find the best system for your own child.

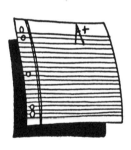

Look-Say Method

Have your child do the following:

1. Pronounce each word carefully.
2. Look carefully at each part of the word as he pronounces it.
3. Say the letters in sequence.
4. Attempt to recall how the word looks, then spell the word.
5. Check this spelling.
6. Write the word.
7. Check the spelling.
8. Repeat these steps.

Visual-Auditory Method (Look-Hear)

Have your child do the following:

1. Say the word
2. Spell the word aloud.
3. Say the word again.
4. Spell the word from memory four times correctly.

Kinesthetic Method (Tracing)

Have your child do the following:

1. Make a model of the word with a crayon or magic marker, saying the word as you make it.

2. Check the accuracy of the model.

3. Trace over the model with his finger, saying the word at the same time.

4. Repeat step 3 five times.

5. Copy the word 3 times correctly.

6. Copy the word 3 times from memory correctly.

> **400 of the most frequently used words children should know how to spell**

There are several good word lists available showing words that are most frequently used in written language. The following list is a compilation of several lists that we have found very useful. If you find that your child is missing any of these basic words, you can use this list. Simply give him a test to find out which words he needs to learn. Then he can study those words using one of our suggested methods.

the	as	but	about	more	now
of	with	what	how	her	people
and	his	all	up	two	my
a	they	were	out	like	made
to	at	when	them	him	over
in	be	we	then	see	did
is	this	there	she	time	down
you	from	can	many	could	find
that	I	an	some	no	use
it	have	your	so	make	day
he	or	which	these	than	water
for	by	if	would	first	long
was	one	do	other	been	little
on	had	will	into	its	very
are	not	each	has	who	after

words	here	might	four	way	usually
called	take	next	head	sentence	money
just	why	sound	above	better	seen
where	things	below	kind	best	fly
most	help	saw	began	across	must
know	put	something	almost	during	didn't
get	years	thought	live	today	car
through	different	both	page	others	morning
back	away	few	got	however	given
much	again	those	earth	sure	bed
before	off	always	need	means	I'm
go	went	locked	far	knew	body
good	old	show	hand	it's	upon
new	number	large	high	try	family
write	great	often	year	told	later
our	tell	together	mother	young	turn
used	men	asked	light	miles	move
me	say	house	parts	sun	face
man	small	don't	country	ways	door
too	every	world	father	dinner	cut
any	found	going	let	whole	done
day	still	want	night	hear	group
same	between	school	following	example	true
right	name	important	picture	heard	half
look	should	until	being	several	sentences
think	Mr.	form	study	change	red
also	home	food	second	answer	fish
around	big	keep	eyes	room	plants
another	give	children	soon	sea	living
came	air	feet	times	against	wanted
come	line	land	story	top	black
work	set	side	boys	turned	eat
three	own	without	since	learn	short
because	under	boy	white	point	United States
does	never	once	days	city	run
part	us	their	ever	play	kinds
even	left	said	paper	toward	book
place	end	enough	hard	five	gave
well	along	took	near	using	order
such	while	sometimes	only	himself	open

ground	I'll	less	certain	list
lines	learned	John	six	stood
cold	brought	wind	feel	hundred
really	close	places	fire	shows
table	nothing	behind	ready	ten
remember	though	cannot	green	fast
tree	started	letter	yes	seemed
read	idea	among	built	felt
last	call	letters	special	kept
course	lived	comes	ran	America
front	makes	able	full	notice
known	became	dog	town	can't
ring	looking	shown	compete	strong
space	add	animals	oh	voice
inside	become	life	person	probably
ago	grow	mean	hot	needed
making	draw	English	anything	birds
Mrs.	yet	rest	hold	
early	hands	perhaps	state	

Additional Resources for Spelling

Downing, David. *303 Dumb Spelling Mistakes and What You Can Do About Them..* National Textbook Company, 1987.

Franklin Speller. Linguistic Technology. Franklin Electronic Speller. Published with Merriam-Webster Dictionary.

Krevisky, Joseph & Jordan L. Linfield. *The Bad Speller's Dictionary.* Random House, 1989.

Moore, George, Richard A. Talbot & G. Willard Woodruff. *Spellex Word Finder.* Curriculum Associates, 1975.

Suid, Murray. *Demonic Mneomonics.* Pitman Learning Inc. 1981.

CHAPTER THREE
WRITING

Writing success depends on constant practice. Your most effective role for helping your child's writing is that of helper, not critic. The following activities will aid your role in improving your child's writing.

Frequency of writing is important. Try to sit down your your youngster as much as possible for practicing writing. Both of you will enjoy this creative time together. Hints for helping your child's writing skills are:

✴ Use any occasion to get your child writing. Ask him to help make a grocery list for the week's shopping. Ask him to write down phone messages—something everyone should learn to do! Encourage good manners as well by having him write thank-you notes and letters to relatives.

✴ Share letters from friends and relatives.

✴ Encourage your youngster to write away for free information, samples, etc.

✴ Praise your child's effort at writing.

✴ Encourage him to write from his own experience. This is one of the most satisfying and successful ways to learn writing. Children love to tell stories of things that have happened to them. If you explain to them that writing is just "talk written down," it makes story writing so much easier.

THREE ACTIVITIES FOR IMPROVED WRITING

Method #1. The Picture File

Step 1. You will need to make a picture file for writing ideas. Cut pictures from newspapers and magazines that will generate ideas for story and paragraph writing. The pictures you save will depend on your child's age and interests. He may be interested in firemen, airplanes, animals, etc.

Step 2. Have your child choose a picture to write about. Have him tell you his story and <u>you</u> write it down <u>exactly</u> as he tells it. An older child might prefer to write his own and then read it to you. You might even type the story—children love to see their stories "in print."

Step 3. When you have finished writing or typing the story, paste it on a piece of construction paper with his picture. Let him check the story to make sure it is exactly the way he wants it.

Step 4. Ask him to read his story aloud to you. It is important to make positive comments about every story. This will build a strong self-image in the youngster.

Step 5. Make a vocabulary card for any word he misses in his reading of the story. Simply put the word on an index card and keep a file where he can go to review the words. You will also want to review the words with him frequently until he knows them. This not only helps him with his writing, but also builds his vocabulary. As his vocabulary increases, his reading and writing will improve dramatically.

Method #2. Easy Paragraphing

The following 6-step method for writing a paragraph can be used with any child from 3rd grade through high school. It can be used on any topic, from your family Thanksgiving to the causes of the American Revolution.

Paragraphs are important building blocks for writing. This method is based on a structured way to develop a main idea, give supporting details, and give a closing sentence. Given the following system, your child will be able to write a paragraph easily after only a little practice.

Step 1. Choose a topic. Example: Thanksgiving.

Step 2. Make a list of words about the topic. List all the details you can remember if it's a specific classroom assignment.
Example: turkey   family   thanks   dressing
          Pilgrims   holiday   dinner   cranberries

Step 3. Write a statement about the topic that tells the main idea. Example: Thanksgiving is my favorite holiday.

Step 4. Your child should pick 3 or 4 words from the word list you made up to use in the paragraph.

Step 5. Your child will write several complete sentences using the words he has picked out. Stress that the sentences should be related to the topic as written in the first sentence.

Step 6. Have him write a closing sentence. This sentence will summarize the ideas in the paragraph. Often it is a rephrasing of the topic sentence.

Method #3. Clustering

Clustering is a relatively new method of teaching writing being used in some schools. It is also called mapping. It is effective because it is visual and gives a child a way of organizing information.

The main idea, or topic, is written in the center of the page. Additional ideas to be included the story are written in a circular fashion around the main theme.

Clustering Key

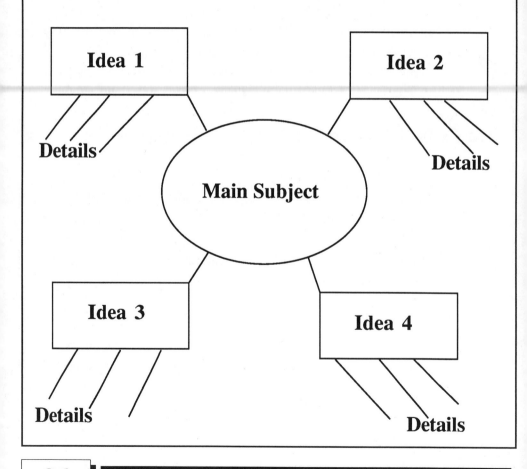

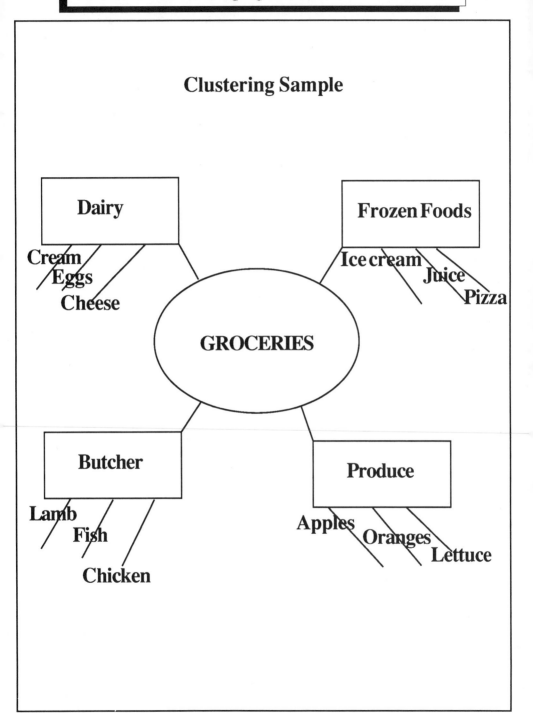

Clustering Sample

Dairy
Cream
Eggs
Cheese

Frozen Foods
Ice cream
Juice
Pizza

GROCERIES

Butcher
Lamb
Fish
Chicken

Produce
Apples
Oranges
Lettuce

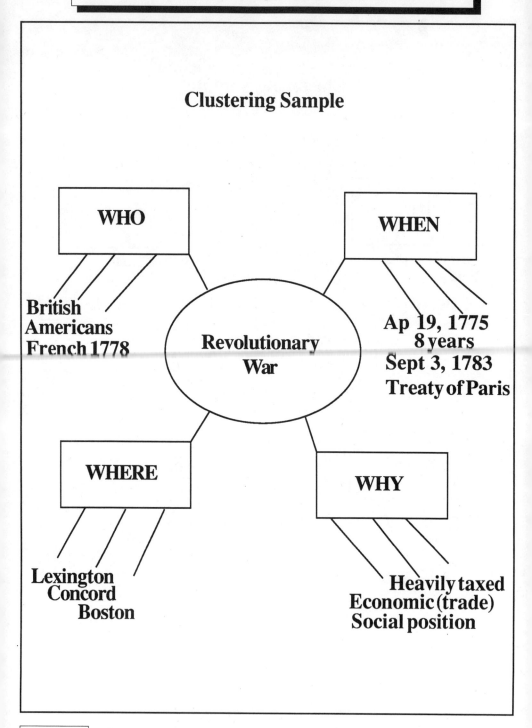

Clustering Sample

WHO

WHEN

British
Americans
French 1778

Revolutionary
War

Ap 19, 1775
8 years
Sept 3, 1783
Treaty of Paris

WHERE

WHY

Lexington
Concord
Boston

Heavily taxed
Economic (trade)
Social position

Additional Resource For Writing

Allen, Roach Van & Claryce. *Language Experience Activities*. Houghton Mifflin, 1982.

Frank, Marjorie. *If You're Trying to Teach Kids How to Write You've Gotta Have This Book*. Incentive Publications, 1979.

Graves, D. H. *Writing: Teachers and Children at Work*. Heinemann Educational Books, 1983.

Hillerich, Robert L. *Teaching Children to Write, K-8*. Prentice-Hall, Inc., 1985.

Rico, Gabriela L. *Writing the Natural Way*. J. P. Tarchers, Inc., 1983.

Sobol, Tom & Harriet. *Your Child in School: Kindergarten Through Second Grade*. Arbor House, 1987.

Sobol, Tom & Harriet. *Your Child in School: The Intermediate Years: Grades Three Through Five*. Arbor House, 1987.

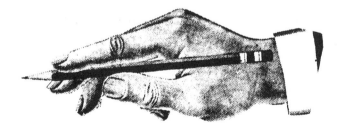

**Many activities, including games,
can be math learning experiences.**

Chapter Four: Math

CHAPTER FOUR
MATH

Math can easily be learned through everyday life experiences. This chapter shows daily activities that parents can use to help their children with math. Together, the family can learn that math is fun, not painful. Math opportunities should always be in natural and meaningful settings. This makes math more fun and builds a foundation of basic mathematical skills that your child can apply to his schoolwork.

✓ One very important note: Never tell your children that "I always hated math." or that "Math always way hard for me." If you start their math experience by telling them that math was a bad experience for you, then they will expect the same for themselves. Instead, try simple math experiences with your child, and adventure into math with a positive attitude. Perhaps you, too, will learn the math is not painful, but rather a simple tool for problem solving.

Activities Group #1: Counting

Counting is something that comes naturally to your child. Youngsters have a natural curiosity about numbers. They love to count and will use counting in a number of different ways. What will you child learn from counting experiences?

> ➥ He will learn how to count.
> ➥ He will learn that numbers stand for specific amounts.
> ➥ He will learn to do simple addition and subtraction.
> ➥ He will learn to estimate "more than" and "less than."

Counting is more than just reciting the numbers in order. It includes matching objects, comparing them, putting them in various positions to see patterns and relationships, and arriving at totals.

Daily activities can be counting experiences. Use fun, familiar, and repetitious situations. Don't lose out on the many chances you and your child have daily to practice counting.

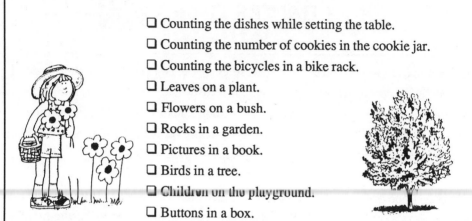

❑ Counting the dishes while setting the table.
❑ Counting the number of cookies in the cookie jar.
❑ Counting the bicycles in a bike rack.
❑ Leaves on a plant.
❑ Flowers on a bush.
❑ Rocks in a garden.
❑ Pictures in a book.
❑ Birds in a tree.
❑ Children on the playground.
❑ Buttons in a box.

To build math skills from the basics of counting, a good tool is Cuisenaire® rods. These are colorful plastic units in many colors and lengths. These can be used to teach addition, subtraction, multiplication, division, and fractions. Children become very proficient and inventive with these rods. When you buy a set of Cuisenaire rods, there are instructions included to show activities for building math skills. The address of the company is at the end of the chapter.

Activities Group #2: Holiday Ideas

The holidays are great times to apply math to life experiences. The family spends more time together, everyone is having fun, and there are extra opportunities for math activities.

Halloween

Count candy to hand out to trick-or-treaters.

Count pumpkin seeds.

Group seeds in piles of 5, 10. Learn multiples of 5.

Estimate the number of pumpkin seeds in a pumpkin patch using multiplication.

Christmas

Add the number of people usually at your dinner table to the number of guests expected. How many in all?

What is the difference between the number of people you usually have for dinner and the number coming?

Count down days to Christmas using calendar or paper chain.

Estimate number of tree ornaments needed.

Count packages under the tree.

Learn the song *The Twelve Days of Christmas*.

New Year's

Count the points on a snowflake.

How many balls would it take to make a snowman? Two snowmen? Ten snowmen?

Valentine's Day

Sort candy by color and count them. Then add the piles together.

How many Valentines cards are needed?

Count the Valentines he receives.

Package up candy in groups of 10 and give to friends. How many pieces did you use in all?

Count the number of hearts he sees on Valentine's Day.

Easter

Count the number of eggs dyed. Subtract how many he colored, how many did someone else color?

Count the number of eggs found on Easter egg hunt. How many children participated? Divide number of eggs by number of children—how many each?

Group jelly beans and candies in Easter baskets to give to friends.

Count the rabbits in a pet store.

Activities Group #3: Money

Your child's first contact with counting money will come from home. As he sees you spending money, he will become interested in learning about it. This is the time to begin teaching him to identify and learn the name of each coin and its value. The next step is to combine coins, so he can learn that different combinations of coins can have the same value. From real-life experiences with money, your child learns:

▲ How to identify coins.

▲ Combinations of coins and the amount they are worth.

▲ Symbols related to money: $ ¢ %

▲ How to make change.

▲ Percentages.

▲ How to write checks.

Money Activity #1: Making a Purchase

One of your child's first money experiences might be a trip to the ice cream parlor. This is an opportunity for him to make a purchase. You can discuss with him the cost and have him choose the coins necessary to pay for his ice cream. You can help him decide which combination of coins he will use to make his purchase.

The grocery store is another great location for learning the relationship between numbers and money. Your youngster will learn more from a trip to the market than he would if you simply sat down with him and worked with coins. He can discover the value of coins, cost of items, and compare prices. He can also add the cost of your grocery bill, subtract the amount from the currency you have, and figure your change. He can see the different symbols used in pricing items. In the meat section he can see the $ and ¢ signs, and in the produce section he will see foods priced according to weight.

Money Activity #2: Making Change

It's Friday night and off to McDonald's® you go. What better way to have your youngster learn about the cost of food than to have him order for the family? Together you can estimate how much he will need to pay the bill. He will also have the chance to see that he gets the correct change back.

In other restaurants, you can have him estimate the cost of the dinner and use percentages to figure out the amount of the tip.

Money Activity #3: Jobs

When your child becomes old enough to do neighborhood jobs such as babysitting or having a paper route, the value of money becomes even more important. This is a good opportunity to help your youngster figure out how many hours he will need to work in order to have enough money to purchase something he wants. In this way, he will use the skills of estimating, adding, multiplying, and dividing.

With a paper route, he must do more sophisticated tasks. He must make change, bill his customers, collect money, and pay his own costs to his company. He must also determine his costs compared to his profits.

Money Activity #4: Checkbook

When your child is old enough to have his own checking account, teach him how to properly record the checks each time he writes one. Show him how to subtract checks written and add deposits. Teach him how to balance a checkbook, and if you're not sure how, learn! Stress accuracy and timeliness—to record each transaction immediately as it occurs, and to balance the checkbook as soon as the statement arrives. This credit-debit system is the basics of accounting, and is no more than adding and subtracting.

Activities Group #4: Time

Time is a concept which you can begin to explore with your child at an early age. What are some of the concepts your child needs to learn about time?

▼Get a feeling for time and its everyday relationship in our lives.

▼Consider the importance of the calendar.

▼Learn to tell the difference between A.M. and P.M.

▼Learn the importance of telling time in order to be on time for school, work, and activities.

▼Become aware of time zones.

Time Activity #1: How long does it take?

Some of the first activities involving time can be to ask these questions:
  ⤷ How long does it take to brush his teeth?

Chapter Four: Math

⤶ How long to take a drink of water?

⤶ Write his name?

⤶ Say the alphabet?

⤶ How long until dinner?

⤶ How long after dinner is his favorite TV show?

⤶ How long before going to bed?

Time Activity #2: Time trivia.

Here are few facts to give your child a sense of time:

❏ 5 seconds: the time it takes thunder to travel 1 mile

❏ 10 minutes: the time it takes a snowflake to form

❏ 15 minutes: a quarter of a football game

❏ 36 hours: a sunflower seed sprouts

❏ 55 days: the Pilgrims crossed the Atlantic

❏ 18 months: a dollar bill wears out

❏ 60 years: the life span of an African elephant

Time Activity #3: Reading the clock.

Ask your youngster to count how many clocks there are in your house. Then ask him to check to see if all the clocks have the same time. This is a good opportunity to compare the standard clock with the popular digital clock. It is important that your child be able to tell time on both types of clocks.

Time Activity #4: Time Zones

It is important for children to learn that when they go from one state to another, across the country, or around the world, they will be entering new time zones. Show your child on his watch what happens from one time zone to another, such as going from east to west, then from west to east. Also explain Daylight Savings Time. When traveling, tell the child when you cross a time zone. These activities can also lead to discussions about geography, climate, and cultures.

The following map shows time zones in the United States:

<u>Time Activity #5: Calendars.</u>

Teach your child that a calendar is a way of counting days and months. Point out the days of the week, the number of weeks in a month, that the number of days in the months change (April 1, April 2, and also March 1, March 2, etc), that twelve months make a year, and that 365 days make a year.

Your child should have his own calendar to mark special activities, homework assignments, and any long-range plans, such as vacations. Show him where the holidays are in relationship to today's date. Let him mark birthdays and count how many months until a certain day. While you're doing this, you can discuss the seasons, the weather, as well as length of time between special occasions.

Activities Group #5: Measurements

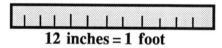

12 inches = 1 foot

There is no better place to introduce your child to measurement than in the kitchen. Both boys and girls love to start helping in the kitchen at an early age. What can your child learn from a cooking experience?

✓ Accuracy in measuring.
✓ Learning to read and follow directions.
✓ Learning that a fraction is a <u>part</u> of something.
✓ Learning about fractional parts, both liquid and solid.
✓ Learning to use different measuring tools: cup, teaspoon, tablespoon, ruler, yardstick, measuring tape.

✓ Using adding, subtracting, and estimating skills.

Measuring Activity #1: Comparing

When cooking in the kitchen, your child needs to do more than just measure. He needs to compare the different amounts as well as relate one to the other. For example: Is 1/2 more or less than 1/4? Is 1/4 plus 1/4 the same as 1/2? In halving or doubling recipes he will also be getting practice with addition and subtraction problems.

Other measuring skills can be learned in the home. Every youngster loves to measure how fast he grows. Pick a spot in your house where your child can either hang a measuring strip or use the wall to mark his height every few months. Then he will be learning how to use a yardstick and a rules. He will become acquainted with the terms feet and inches, and their fractional parts. He will compare his growth from one month to the next, and estimate how much he may grow by the next time he measures himself.

Measuring Activity #2: Larger units of measure

As children grow older, their experiences broaden. They may become interested in which cars go faster, which piece of cake is larger, how far it is to Grandma's, and how many miles they travel on vacation. These new interests provide you with an opportunity to introduce new skills, such as size, distance, and map skills.

Have your child compute the number of miles to your destination when you make a trip. This will help him develop estimating skills and map reading.

When fixing up the house, have your child measure the window size for new curtains. Let him compute how many yards of material it will take. Explain that material comes in different widths, and that you must be prepared to compute for the different widths. When his room needs new furniture, let him draw a scale diagram of his room and show where the new pieces will fit.

ADDITIONAL RESOURCES FOR MATH

Cuisenaire products available from: Cuisenaire Company of America, Inc., 12 Church St., Box D, New Rochelle NY 10802. (914) 235-0900.

Aten, Jerry. *Prime Time Life Skills*. Good Apple, Inc., 1983.

Aten, Jerry. *Prime Time Math Skills*. Good Apple, Inc., 1983.

Baratta-Lorton, Mary. *Workjobs*. Addison-Wesley, 1972.

Burk, Donna and Allyn Snider & Paula Symonds. *Box It or Bag It*. Math Learning Center, 1988.

Burns, Marilyn. *This Book is About Time*. Little, Brown, 1978.

Fisk, Sally. *Learning to Measure*. Milliken Publishing Company, 1985.

Forte, Imogene & Joy MacKenzie. *Creative Math Experiences*, Incentive Publications, 1973.

Gelman, R. & C. R. Gallistel. *The Child's Understanding of Numbers*, Harvard University Press, 1978.

Hart, Jane. *Let's Think About Time*. Hart Publishing Company, 1965.

Kaplan, Sandra and JoAnn Burton Kaplan, Sheila Madsen, & Bette K. Taylor. *Change for Children: Ideas and Activities for Individualizing Learning*. Goodyear Publishing Company, 1973.

Sobol, Tom & Harriet. *Your Child in School: Kindergarten Through Second Grade*. Arbor House, 1987.

Sobol, Tom & Harriet. *Your Child in School: The Intermediate Years: Grades Three Through Five*. Arbor House, 1987.

Young, Eleanor R. *Basic Skills Around the House*. CEBCO Standard Publishing, 1974.

CHAPTER FIVE
HOMEWORK

Parents can help their children be more successful in school by helping them organize their homework time. Good study skills lead to many skills that are useful in other areas of life.

Successful students are motivated students. Motivating your child to succeed in school means helping him perceive himself as a successful student. Self-motivation is one of the most important factors in achieving success in school. Children who fail tend to feel that they have no control over their grades. For children to want to put time and effort into studying, they must believe that the hours spent studying will make a difference between success or failure in school.

Students must learn to accept responsibility for some of their own learning. They need to understand that you are there to support and help them, but ultimately learning is up to them. As the child achieves more success, his self-image and attitude toward school will become more positive.

The learning process is a joint effort. Given consistent study time, methods for learning, and aids for remembering information, your child <u>can</u> improve his grades! As parents, you can make a difference by:

> ★ Showing interest in your child's day-to-day activities. This keeps you informed and encourages good work habits and a positive attitude toward learning.

★ Informing your child's teacher of any problems that may arise. If a problem arises between scheduled conferences, don't hesitate to call for a special meeting. This way you can work together in the best interest of your child.

★ Viewing the teacher as an ally and friend who is as interested in your child's success as you are.

It is important for your child to develop good study skills: an appropriate place to study; a specific time to study; and organizing materials. The place where he studies should have a desk or a table where he can put his materials. It should also have a good light so he can see clearly. Each child should also have a special time that he studies. It might be right after school, before or after dinner. But it's important to study before it's too late in the evening for him to do a good job on his assignments. If possible, he should pick the same time each day for study.

For the older child, establishing a consistent monitoring system of his assignments, test dates, and projects or papers due is a necessary means of assuring he feels successful in school.

Ask your child to show you his assignment sheets daily. He can use a small notebook listing all of the assignments due in every class each day. Students who come to class prepared are more involved in the class and consistently do better in school.

Good study skills teach your child critical life skills:

☞ time management
☞ individual responsibility
☞ self-discipline
☞ motivation

Work Area

The first thing you need to do with your child is to choose an appropriate work space. This area must be quiet and free from distractions.

1. Select a desk or table. This alone helps concentration and helps the child to focus on what is to be done.

2. Pick a quiet location. It should be away from distractions such as TV, radio, stereo, telephone, and people talking.

3. Make sure that there is good lighting. Poor lighting interferes with concentration and causes eye strain.

4. For younger children or those experiencing difficulty in school, you will want to have the work area near you. This will allow you to be available for help.

5. Provide needed supplies such as pencils, pencil sharpener, pen, paper, scratch pads, hole punch, and a dictionary so your child won't have to get up and down each time he needs something. We also suggest a book stand. This eliminates holding a book, leaving the student free to take notes. It also makes him feel professional, and adds pizzazz to the work place! Use the checklist below.

Things I Need When I Study	Dates I Checked My Materials								
MATERIALS:									
Books									
Paper									
Notebook									
Assignments									
Pens									
Pencils									
Eraser									
Dictionary									
Book stand									

Study Time

Work out a planned study time for each day. It should include a specific starting time and a specific length of time to study. This will eliminate rushing through his homework and will encourage him to remember to bring assignments home. It will also eliminate the dreaded "I forgot my homework" syndrome!

If he finishes early or has no homework, use the scheduled time for extra reading, studying, spelling or vocabulary, reviewing basic math facts, or going over previously learned material.

1. Pick the same time each day, if possible. It is a good idea for the child to have adult supervision during study time.

2. Work out together when studying will be done. Use the Student Planning Worksheet that follows.

3. A rule of thumb is ten minutes per day per grade level. Each day estimate the amount of time needed to complete each assignment and plan for it. A

good way to learn to estimate is to watch the amount of time your child usually takes to do a certain type of assignment.

4. Once the specific study time is determined, fill the times on the Homework Contract. Post it near his study area.

HOMEWORK CONTRACT

Talk with your parents to help you set up a time and a place to study. Fill out the following contract. Good luck!

I, _____, am going to make a special effort to use my time and place to study.
The place I will study is _____.
This place has a desk or table, has good lighting, and is quiet.

The times I will study are:

Monday: _____
Tuesday: _____
Wednesday: _____
Thursday: _____
Friday: _____
Weekend (if needed): _____

_____   _____
Student's Signature   Parent's Signature

_____
Date

Notebooking

Provide your child with a notebook where he can organize his assignments. Students are more apt to get assignments to and from school if they have a <u>single</u> notebook to be responsible for. This notebook can be organized subject-by-subject and have the work all in one place.

1. Choose a backpack or bookbag for carrying work to and from school.

2. In the lower grades, help your child organize a folder or notebook for homework materials.

3. In the upper grades, help your child organize a notebook with dividers by subject areas, paper, zipper pouch for pencil, pens, eraser, etc, and a homework assignment sheet.

4. See the Notetaking Chapter on additional advantages of notebooking.

Assignment Sheets

Student achievement rises significantly when they regularly complete homework because the total time spent studying is directly related to how much he learns. Assignment sheets help him become responsible for organizing his homework, which in turn teaches him organizational skills and time management.

1. Homework assignments should be written down on an assignment sheet. Older students sometimes prefer to use a small notebook to write in their daily assignments. Use whatever works for your child, but try to make it as organized as possible.

2. The student can use the "Comments" column on the sample Weekly Assignment Sheet to remind himself of other things to do. It could be used

WEEKLY ASSIGNMENT SHEET

Week of _____	Monday	Tuesday	Wednesday	Thursday	Friday
Reading					
Math					
Spelling					
Social Studies					
Science					
Other					

for upcoming tests, teacher comments, or prioritizing homework.

3. Writing the correct information on his assignment sheet or notebook is as important as doing the homework. If he doesn't know what he is supposed to do and doesn't know the page numbers, the homework assignment will be incomplete.

4. Go over his assignments. Which one is hardest? Which one is easiest? Together, number the order he decided to do them. A good rule is to begin with the hardest, because a person is at his best when he is just starting.

5. Review your child's assignment daily. Be sure give praise for completion of work.

Additional Resources for Homework

Black, Ginger E. *Making the Grade: A+ Advice for Parents.* Carol Publishing Group, 1989.

Canter, Lee & Lee Hausner. *Homework Without Tears.* Harper Row, 1988.

Devine, Thomas. *Guidebook for Teaching Study Skills and Motivation.* Allyn & Bacon, 1982.

Devine, Thomas & Linda D. Meagher. *Mastering Study Skills: A Student Guide.* 1989.

Fields, Terri. *How to Help Your Child Make the Most of School.* Villard Books, 1987. Fisher Books, 1989.

Gall, Meredith D. & Joyce D. *Making the Grade.* Prima Publishing & Communications, 1988.

CHAPTER SIX
MEMORY

It is common knowledge that everyone forgets most of what he or she learns. Psychologists say that after four weeks we have forgotten 98% of what we have read in newspapers, heard in conversations, or seen on television. Because memory tends to be a common problem for children that are experiencing difficulty in school, this chapter shows methods to strengthen memory.

People have different learning styles. People learn through their senses: taste, touch, smell, hearing, and sight. More learning comes from sight than from all the other senses combined. Learning can be strengthened by using several senses. Thus memory strategies are often combinations of the senses.

All people can benefit by learning memory strategies, but students experiencing difficulty in school can be particularly helped by them:

1. They often have difficulty passing a test. Since tests are requirements of formal learning, and since tests make up a large part of their grade, memory improvement helps grades.

2. These students tend to be passive rather than active learners due to the fact that they don't know how to memorize information.

3. These students may exhibit anxiety and lack of motivation toward tests because they haven't learned effective methods for memorizing information.

There's some basic points to remember about memory. First, for the average child, short-term memory functions best in the morning, so a quick cramming early in the day is effective. Second, long-term memory seems to work best in the late afternoon and evenings. Third, reviewing information within 24 hours of the first study session is the most effective way to master any material. Fourth, repetition enhances memory.

The following memory methods have worked well for many people, not only students. They are time-tested and worth the effort to learn. Basically, they're just little "tricks" to jog your memory. You may have even used these methods without even realizing it.

Memory Method #1: Acronyms

An acronym is a word formed from the initials of other words. For example: AMA is an acronym for the American Medical Association. USA is an acronym for the United States of America. HOME is an acronym for Home Offering Meaningful Education (an organization).

Lists of things you want to memorize can be formed into acronyms. Sometimes it is difficult to create a real word that is associated with the information, but you can invent a word. Just be sure that you remember the word!

For example, the words SHARP CUBE could be used as an acronym to recall the names of the Eastern Block countries. Try this:

S	Soviet Union
H	Hungary
A	Albania
R	Rumania
P	Poland
C	Czechoslovakia
U	Yugoslavia
B	Bulgaria
E	East Germany

Another examples is the word HOMES. This acronym could be used to trigger your memory to recall the names of the five Great Lakes:

H	Huron
O	Ontario
M	Michigan
E	Erie
S	Superior

Memory Method #2: Rhyming

This method is commonly used to learn series, terms, or groups of words. An example is this familiar rhyme:

> Thirty days has September
> April, June, and November.
> Thirty-one all the rest rate,
> Except for February, which has twenty-eight.

Remember these rhymes from grade school?

> Columbus sailed the ocean blue
> In fourteen hundred ninety-two.

> i before e except after c
> or when sounding like a
> as in neighbor and weigh.

> Artery beings with "a"
> From the heart it takes blood away.
> Vein has at its end an "n"
> It take the blood back again.

Create silly rhymes to help your child remember lists or special rules.

Memory Method #3: Visualization

Visualization is a technique where you see something in your mind without really seeing it. This is one of the most easily used and most effective techniques for children of all ages who are trying to recall a specific piece of information.

The brain is divided into left and right hemispheres. The left side stores verbal information; the right stores visual information. When trying to remember facts and ideas, combining a word with a picture uses both sides of your brain, and is a powerful way to empower memory.

For example, if you need to remember that Abraham Lincoln was born in 1809 in a log cabin, picture a log cabin with the date 1809 over the doorway:

In science, you might need to remember that crabs are crustaceans. Picture a crab holding or eating a crust of bread!

New vocabulary words can be learned using this method. Take the word <u>barrister</u>. The word you choose to associate with it should sound as much like the vocabulary word as possible. <u>Bear</u> has sounds in common with <u>barrister</u>. That is your first link. The second link is a visual one. The student can make a mental picture of a bear in a suit acting like a lawyer. For each vocabulary word, the child can develop a similar or rhyming word with a mental picture. Later, when the student is studying the vocabulary word, he will remember the linking word, and then will visualize the picture with the word.

There have been studies where students used this technique to study 14 difficult vocabulary words for 8 minutes. Those using this technique remembered 82% of the definitions while those not using the method recalled only 21%!

This method can also be used for remembering series of numbers. The following example is from the book *The Sixth Sense: Practical Tips for Everyday Safety* by Joseph Niehaus (available from Blue Bird Publishing, order form in back of this book.) For remembering the series 3 8 5 6 2 9, try visualizing the following. Imagine the 3 floating around in the air, and the 8 comes long and hooks itself to the bottom on the 3. Now the 5 comes along and spears the bottom loop of the 8 with its hat. The 5 is then hooked on the bottom by the hook of the 6. The 6 rocks back and forth as it rests on the 5. The 2 drops down and hooks the loop of the 6. Then the 9 links up with the bottom leg of the 2.

It's the image the helps you remember the numbers. The more creative the image, the easier it is to remember.

Memory Method #4: Linking

Using a sentence or silly story to link ideas is another technique for remembering information. Make up a silly sentence using the first letter of each word we want to recall.

For geography:

Try to remember the 7 continents of the world. They are Asia, Africa, Antarctica, Australia, Europe, South America, and North America. Use the beginning letters of this simple sentence and see how easy it becomes: **A**lice **A**te **A**n **A**pple **E**very **S**aturday **N**ight.

In science:

Students find it easy to remember the names of the planets by a simple sentence. In order from the sun they are: Mercury, Venus, Earth, Mars, Jupiter, Saturn, Uranus, Neptune, Pluto.
Men **V**ery **E**asily **M**ake **J**ugs **S**erve **U**seful and **N**umerous **P**urposes.

With spelling:

This technique also works well when having to spell a long but commonly used word such as <u>arithmetic</u>:
A **R**at **I**n **T**he **H**ouse **M**ight **E**at **T**he **I**ce **C**ream.

For social studies:

A simple sentence has been very useful for teaching children the names of the original thirteen colonies. Although not every word stands for a state, and some of the strategy comes from "stretching" the technique just a little, it really works:

DE   MD CT   GA   MA

Dell and **Mar**y **c**ame from **Georgia** and **Massachusetts**

VA RI   PA   3 N's: NJ, NY, NH

to **v**isit **Ri**chard and **Penn**y and their three **n**ephews

NC   SC

from **North Carolina** and **South Carolina**.

For math:

To remember a series of numbers, create a story using the numbers as a key. This example is from the book *The Sixth Sense: Practical Tips for Everyday Safety* by Joseph Niehaus (available from Blue Bird Publishing, order form in back of this book.) To remember the series 3 8 5 6 2 9, try this story:

Once upon a time there were 3 bears. The 3 bears lived 8 houses down from the beach. One day the bears decided to walk 5 miles. The packed 6 bottles of juice for the trip. They took 2 pairs of sunglasses and left the house at 9 a.m.

Memory Method #5: Association

Association is the process where you associate an idea or fact you need to remember with something you already know. You can use your imagination and previous knowledge to form a memory chain with the new information that you want to recall. To associate means "to go together." When you use the association technique you think of some way in which the things you want to remember go together.

For example, if you met a man named Mr. Perkins and you want to remember his name the next time you meet, you could use the association technique. You might visualize a perking coffee pot and the aroma of freshly-brewed coffee. You are tying in your previous knowledge (perking coffee) with Mr. Perkin's name.

You may have learned that it is easy to remember how to spell <u>piece</u> if you think of the phrase, <u>a piece of pie</u>. Since <u>pie</u> is an easy word to spell, by associating this "old knowledge" with the new, you can easily spell <u>piece</u>.

Not many people can remember the shape of France or Russia, but everyone can remember how Italy is shaped. That's because early in school we learned that Italy is shaped like a boot. We associate the shape of the boot (old knowledge) with Italy (new knowledge) and we never forget its shape because of the association between the two.

By making a silly picture, we can use our imagination to form a mental image of what we're trying to remember. Often, the more ridiculous the image, the more likely we are to remember the information. Read the following nonsense story. See how long it takes you to learn the names of all the U.S. Presidents in order. (Source: *30 Ways to Improve Your Grades,* by Harry Shaw.)

Adam (<u>Adams</u>) was the first man but the second President after Washington. These two had a little dog named Jeff (<u>Jefferson</u>) who went mad (<u>Madison</u>). The got the "mon" (money, <u>Monroe</u>) and took him to the vet, Dr. <u>Adams</u>. The vet took their "jack" (money, <u>Jackson</u>) and put it in a van. (<u>Van Buren</u>). He then grabbed his son Harry (<u>Harrison</u>), tied (<u>Tyler</u>) him in a poke (<u>Polk</u>), and took him to a tailor (<u>Taylor</u>). The tailor's shop was filled (<u>Fillmore</u>) with stuff, but he calmly kept on piercing (<u>Pierce</u>) a buckskin (<u>Buchanan</u>) with his needle. He then got his <u>Lincoln</u> out of the garage, called his son, John (<u>Johnson</u>), and drove off without granting (<u>Grant</u>) a hello (<u>Hayes</u>) to his wife who was in the fields (<u>Garfield</u>). They picked up a boy named <u>Arthur</u> and drove toward <u>Cleveland</u>, where they stayed in the Hotel <u>Harrison</u> outside of <u>Cleveland</u>.

Then they set off for Mt. <u>McKinley</u>, where they saw <u>Roosevelt</u> leading a group up behind the slopes with fat <u>Taft</u> lumbering behind. They couldn't see <u>Wilson</u> very well because it was hard

(<u>Harding</u>) to make thing out in the cool (<u>Coolidge</u>) fog. So they left and went on to the <u>Hoover</u> Dam, on which they saw sitting a man with a cigarette holder in his mouth (<u>Roosevelt</u>), a true man (<u>Truman</u>), a fellow named Ike (<u>Eisenhower</u>), a youngster named Ken (<u>Kennedy</u>), and a boy named John (<u>Johnson</u>) who kept saying "nix" (<u>Nixon</u>). Then they drove home in a <u>Ford</u> with a cart (<u>Carter</u>) behind them It was hard to drive because <u>Reagan</u> was afraid of running into the <u>Bush</u>.

Additional Resources For Memory

Bienstock, Eric M. *Success Through Better Memory*. Putnam Publishing Company, 1989.

Bornstein, Arthur. *How to Improve Your Memory*. Audio cassette. Listen USA, 1984.

Buzan, Tony. *Use Your Perfect Memory*. E.P. Dutton, 1984.

Lapp, Danielle C. *Don't Forget: Easy Exercises for a Better Memory at Any Age*. McGraw-Hill Book Company, 1987.

Lorayne, Harry & Jerry Lucas. *The Memory Book*. Ballantine Books, 1974.

Minninger, Joan. *Total Recall: How to Boost Your Memory Power*. Rodale Press, 1984.

Reid, Struan. *Improve Your Memory Skills*. Usborne Publishers Ltd., 1988.

Shaw, Harry. *30 Ways to Improve Your Grades*. McGraw-Hill, 1976.

CHAPTER SEVEN
NOTETAKING

Notetaking helps students learn because while they are writing, they are active learners. Notetaking also enables your child to maintain concentration on the task at hand. It provides a method for gathering and recording information. His notes then become a source for retrieving the information needed to answer questions in class and for studying for a test. Even though notetaking may seem a tedious task, in the long run it is a timesaver in that he will not need to go back to look up an answer or reread all of the material for a test.

There are different types of notes and ways of taking them down, depending on the material to be learned.

1. In definition-type notes, the information to be learned consists of new vocabulary, which goes on the left side of the paper, and the definition, which goes beside it on the right side of the paper.

2. The topic-and-idea type notes contain information on a given subject. A topic is introduced which is written on the left side and expanded information on the topic is written on the right.

3. The paragraph-type notes are those pulled out of the textbook. Information is recorded with the main idea on the left and details on the right.

Cornell/Two-Column Notetaking System

This is a simple and effective method for taking and reviewing notes. It provides the student with notes that can be used to answer chapter questions, for daily review, and as a study guide for tests. Once your child has learned to use this system with written material, he can also used the same format to take notes on class lectures.

Step 1. Use a loose-leaf notebook because it allows your child to insert handouts and assignment sheets. It also enables him to have a section for each subject in which he has notes readily available to him. It also makes it easy to add additional paper and notes to each subject area.

Step 2. While learning this system, have him fold the sheets of paper in half vertically. That forms two columns. For easiest review, write only on one side of the paper.

Step 3. At the top of the left column write "Main Idea" and on the top of the right column write "Details."

Paragraph-by-Paragraph Notetaking Method

Since most students are gaining information from a textbook, the following is application of the Cornell/ Two-Column Notetaking System to textbook reading. Most writers present one main idea per paragraph, so your child is more apt to succeed if he reads one paragraph at a time and takes notes on it.

Step 1. Have your child read the first paragraph thorough enough to answer the question: "What is this paragraph about?" He should record this on the left column using only key words (usually one to three words). If he is unable to answer the question, have him reread the paragraph until he can. Number the paragraphs.

Step 2. He should ask himself the question, "What are the important facts or details about the main idea?" He should record that information on the right column across from the main idea. This may consist of two or three lines. It is important that he put this in his own words. Skip a line before starting on the next paragraph.

Step 3. He should do this for each paragraph until he reaches the end of the chapter. When he finishes, he will find that not only does he have the necessary information to answer the questions at the end of the chapter, but he also has a study guide for the test.

Using Notes to Study for a Test

The next steps will show how to use these notes for reviewing for a test. Keep in mind that daily review of notes, or at least the most recent notes, will build a long-term memory for these items. Then just before the test, you can apply extra test-taking systems to improve scores dramatically.

Read | Have your child read the first page of his notes. Have him read these notes as many times as necessary until he knows the material without looking at it.

Recall | He should now fold back the notebook paper so that he is only looking at the Main idea column. After reading the first main idea, he should be able to recall the Detail information. If he can do this, then he has mastered the material. If he can't, then he should go back to the "READ" step and reread the information. He shouldn't fall into the trap of believing that rereading takes the place of reciting. Only when he can recall aloud the Detail side to you has he truly mastered the material.

CORNELL NOTETAKING SYSTEM
Paragraph by Paragraph Reading Method

① Vikings come to Russia	During Middle Ages moved up rivers to forest boats light - carry
② Landscape change	left forest Vast grassland (steppes)
③ Slavs	1st tribes live E. Europe / log homes
④ Slavs traded	beeswax - candles polish marble
⑤ Rurik	862, Vikings settled on river leader of Novgorod brother settled Kiev
⑥ Descendant of Rurik	Princes of Russian towns for centuries.

Chapter Seven: Notetaking

Review   This step requires that he open the whole paper and check his answers. If he can remember all the information correctly, he should go on and memorize the next page. If he forgets something that is important, then he should study that item until he can recall it without reading.

Successful notetaking and reviewing using this system will result in dramatic improvement in grades if followed faithfully. These are systems that good students have used without even realizing why their grades were so good.

Repetition + Review = Success in School.

Additional Resources on Notetaking

Carnine, Douglas, Jerry Silbert & Edward J. Kameenui. *Direct Instruction Reading.* Second Edition, Merrill Publishing Company, 1990.

Jensen, Eric. *Student Success Secrets.* Barron's Educational Series, 1982.

Staff of the Communication & Learning Center. *125 Ways to be a Better Student.* LinguiSystems, Inc., 1986.

Tracey, Anne C. *How to Study.* Modern Curriculum Press, 1970.

CHAPTER EIGHT
TEST-TAKING

Your child may be one of those people whose palms begin to sweat at the mere mention of a test! School will probably always involve taking tests, but test-taking will become easier if he knows how to prepare for them. There are test-taking secrets that better students have always used, sometimes without even realizing that they had discovered a method. Sometimes "average" students were simply the ones who had not yet discovered test-taking secrets. All students who use a system to study for a test will bring home better grades. You can teach your child a system, and you can see that he is prepared, rested, relaxed, and ready to do his best!

Test Preparation

☆ <u>Review notes</u>. The last chapter shows how to review notes. There should be intense, concentrated studying at this point. A parent might wonder how much time should a student study for a test? It's hard to put a numerical measure on this, since there are so many variables. But the student should know his notes by heart and should be able to answer most of the questions a parent would ask about textbook material. If there's three days before the test, the student should put in time <u>before</u> the last day preceding the test. The day preceding the test should be spent in last-minute reviews of the <u>hardest</u> material, such as concentrated memorization of lists. This is the time to use memory methods to learn long lists of material.

Repeat the memory techniques (like silly sentences) over and over until you know your child will not forget them! And remember what they stand for. Remind you child to review these hardest things minutes before the test, just to be sure he is ready.

★ Review textbook material. Have your child reread the most important and hardest material. If he owns the books, and has highlighted the important points as he read them, then concentrate on the highlighted areas. Make sure he knows by heart the new definitions of terms—these are almost always asked in a test. He must know the overall theme of the material, and how it applies in particular instances. If there's names and dates to be remembered, try setting up a matching quiz, with names or dates on one side, and the important details about them on the other. This is a good way to review them. Lists must also be memorized, using memory techniques when necessary. It helps when a parent reviews with a child, even an older child, because the child knows immediately if he is right or wrong. And he can study harder the material he has missed.

★ Analyze the teacher. This may sound odd, but some of the best students know that they have to figure out what the teacher wants in order to be ready for it. If this is the first test from this teacher, then you have to try to guess what type of material he will put on the test. Think about what he has stressed in class. Has he stressed definitions? Dates? People? Analytical material? Has he strayed from the textbook material frequently? If allowed, look at exams he has given in the past. If there has been a previous test, look at the types of material included. You will definitely be better prepared if you know what to expect from this particular teacher—and then be prepared for anything!!

☆ <u>Get a good night's sleep</u>. Before a test, <u>always</u> be sure your child is rested. The hardest study should be finished the day before the exam. There's evidence that if a person studies something very intensely, and then gets a good rest, that the material will be learned better. The day of the exam, lighter review is good. And minutes before the exam, it's best to review the hardest-to-remember items, like lists. Remind your college-age kids that partying is a no-no the night before an exam!

☆ <u>Eat a high protein breakfast</u>. In fact, try to see that your child always has a nutritious breakfast for best school performance.

☆ <u>Dress comfortably</u>.

☆ <u>Bring all necessary materials to class</u>—pens, pencils, paper, notes, brain, etc.

☆ <u>Be on time</u>.

☆ <u>Relax</u>. While this may seem odd—studying intensely and then telling the child to relax before the exam—it <u>is</u> effective! Tell your child that if he is nervous, take a few deep breaths and think about something pleasant. Teach him how to put his mind in a comfortable, relaxed mood. He will do his best on tests if he is prepared, yet relaxed.

☆ <u>Put everything else out of your mind and think of doing only your best</u>. Prepare, relax, do your best. It's a system that really works!

Test-Taking Tips

1. Before you take the test, find out as much as you can about it. Will

it be essay, multiple choice, true-false, matching, or fill-in? How many points is each question worth?

2. Skim over the entire test before answering any questions. The purpose of this is to see how the test is composed. It might begin with essay questions, then have multiple choice, and then a few fill-in. Get an idea of where the most points are located, and do those problems first. For example, if the test is 50 points, and three essay questions are worth 35 points, this is the bulk of the test, and effort should be given accordingly.

3. Watch the time and budget it according to the number of problems and their point value.

4. Be sure you understand all the directions on the test. Ask for clarification if you do not understand the directions. Be sure to follow the directions, and answer according to the question asked.

5. Answer all the questions you can, skipping those that are difficult the first time through. Don't ponder over the hard questions now, that would be wasting time. Use your time wisely and get the most questions right that you are sure you know. Then go back and do the harder questions. Mark the questions you skip so that you can find them quickly when you go back.

6. Remember that information in one question may give you a clue, or even the answer, to another question. This is another reason for skimming the test first.

7. Remember if you are not certain of the answer, your first impression is usually best. If your intuition is telling you an answer is correct, it could be that the right side of your brain is probably at

work and it could be right.

8. Don't assume that your teacher has based the answers on any pattern. For instance, if you think your teacher is planning True-False answers to go: T T F F T T F F, don't bet on it! Your teacher does not have time to make a test based on the pattern of the answers.

Types of Tests

True-False:

      * When words such as <u>always</u>, <u>never</u>, <u>all</u> and <u>must</u> are used, the answer will often be false.

      * When qualifying words such as <u>sometimes</u>, <u>usually</u>, <u>might</u>, and <u>most</u> are used, the answer is usually true.

      * There will often be more true answers than false ones since teachers would rather leave true information with the students.

      * If you don't know the answer, it's a good idea to guess at answers because you have a 50% chance of getting them right.

Multiple Choice:

      * Be sure to watch whether the question asks for "the best answer" or "all correct answers."

      * Use the process of elimination to increase your chance at getting a correct answer. Read all the choices. Cross out the answers that you know are <u>not</u> correct. Choose the best answer from the ones left.

✳ If you must guess, try these hints:

✓Longest multiple choice answers are best guesses.

✓If questions have 5 possible choices, pick the one that says "All of the Above."

✓"None of the Above" is a poor choice.

✓If two out of four choices are similar, pick the longest of the two.

✓When an answer contains an absolute word, such as never, all, always, totally, none, etc., choose the answer that does not contain these words.

Matching:

✳ Always begin with the top item in the left column until you find a match for it in the right column. Read down the entire right column to be sure that your answer is the best match. If you're not sure, skip to the next item and come back to it later.

✳ Continue down the left column, filling in the matches you're sure of.

✳ As you use an answer in the right column, check it off so you don't need to keep rereading it.

✳ Go back and fill in any items you skipped. Guess if you must.

✳ Be careful. In some matching tests, the same answer may be used more than once. Read directions to be sure.

Fill-In Questions:

* Begin with the easiest questions and fill in the blanks.

* Don't waste time on questions if you don't know the answer. Go back to those questions later.

* Never leave a question blank. Guess. You might get partial credit for being close.

Essay:

* Write clear, precise answers. Don't beat around the bush, but get right to the point. Write in paragraph form, with the main idea first, then details and supporting facts.

* Notice the most important words in the directions, such as compare, contrast, discuss, list, etc. Then do exactly what the directions say.

* Start with the easiest question.

* Plan your answers by jotting down important facts or a short outline in the margin (if allowed) or on scratch paper.

* Budget your time carefully. An essay test is the easiest one to forget the time element. If there's 5 questions for an hour exam, that's 12 minutes each. Spend that amount on a question and go on. You can always return to add details if you have time left in the hour.

* Be neat and legible. Even though you feel that you must rush to put down all the material necessary for a

correct answer, it's important for the teacher to be able to read your answer. Fuzzy writing may decrease your score.

Additional Resources for Test-Taking

Bautista, Veltisezar B. *Improve Your Grades*. Bookhaus Publishers, 1988.

Fry, Ronald W. *How to Study*. Career Press, Inc., 1989.

Greene, Lawrence & Leigh Jones-Bomman. *Getting Smarter*. David S. Lake Publisher, 1985.

Lengefeld, Uelaine. *Study Skill Strategies*. Crisp Publications, Inc., 1986.

Olney, Claude. *Where There's A Will There's An A*. American Educational Publications, 1988. Audio and video cassettes available with handbook.

Staff of the Communication and Learning Center. *125 Ways to be a Better Student*. LinguiSystems., 1986.

PART TWO

FAMILY TALK & READ SESSIONS

WHAT ARE FAMILY TALK & READ SESSIONS?

Family Talk & Read sessions are a unique method for improving children's reading and oral skills. The purpose of these sessions is to help improve their speech, their pronunciation of words while storytelling and reading, and to increase their enthusiasm for storytelling and reading. It's also an entertaining way to spend time together as a family!

The first family session is probably the most important, because it sets the tone for those that follow. It also helps determine whether the children's attitude toward this activity will be positive or negative. If the right atmosphere is established—one that is relaxed and good-natured—and the children are praised and not criticized for their efforts, the chances are they'll enjoy the meeting and look forward to the next one. Your aim should be to creative this kind of positive atmosphere.

Careful preparation on your part can help make it a success. The first question to decide is: Which evening will you choose for your family meeting? You, the parents, must talk this over by yourselves, because you will want to choose a night that conflicts least with the children's TV watching, and perhaps your own, too. If their favorite program is on Thursday evening, then stay away from Thursday. Choose another night. Once you have settled on a night, it would be best to stay with it. Don't keep changing from one night to another unnecessarily; it could cause arguments and undermine the program.

There's no need to announce at this first meeting that you intend to make this a weekly event. Just go ahead and meet, have an enjoyable time, and hopefully the suggestion will come from the children to have another meeting.

If you have only one or two children, your task of leading the sessions will be quite easy. If you have three or more children, it will be more of a challenge, but still not really that difficult. You'll simply need a bit more forethought and preparation before each meeting. In either case, you will need to plan your first two meetings carefully, as to launch the program successfully.

The program that is presented here will suggest a variety of approaches to be used with children of different ages. You can consider these and decide which are best suited to your own situation. You may even be able to think of others that will work better. A lot depends on your children's ages and on the rapport that exists among you.

Naturally, you know your children better than anyone else does. You are clearly aware of their individual personalities, their idiosyncrasies, their likes and dislikes, their talents, how well they get along with each other, etc. Thus you are in a position to know what ideas and techniques will work best with them.

There are other factors that operate here, such as the children's attitudes toward books and reading. If they like books, and if you have read to them a great deal and they now enjoy reading for themselves, then they will adapt quickly to these sessions. If you've always had books in the house and you enjoy reading, your children will tend to follow your lead and become interested in books as well.

In the same way, if you have encouraged family discussion, then the children will tend to enjoy their speaking part of the sessions. The parent who has regularly taken time to talk with each child, to answer his questions, to exchange thoughts and ideas, will have an easier time guiding the sessions than the parent who does this only rarely.

Generally, the younger the children are, and the closer together in ages, the easier it will be to begin a program like this. Seven-year-olds will take to it more readily than 12-year-olds. However, if your children happen to be in the older age range, don't let that put a damper on your enthusiasm. They will enjoy the program once it gets started. You may need to use a bit more subtlety in the way you present the idea to them.

Younger children are not so apt to protest to question your announcement: "We're going to try something different tonight after supper. It's called 'Talk & Read,' and it's for the whole family. We'll all sit together in the living room and take turns talking and reading to each other. We're going to play a couple of games we've never played before, and also tell some jokes and riddles. It's going to be fun..."

Don't explain too much in advance. In this way the children's curiosity and interest will be sustained. Now let's get started....

CHAPTER NINE:

FAMILY TALK & READ SESSION ONE
RIDDLES, JOKES & SILLY STORIES

Purpose:

To improve oral communication

To improve enunciation (clear pronunciation of speech)

To create enthusiasm for storytelling

To improve listening skills

To encourage impromptu speech

This is your first Family Talk & Read session. The atmosphere should be light and friendly. This night will be fun. For this first night, there will not need to be heavy preparation.

Just ask each child to bring some of his favorite jokes and riddles. Most children know some riddles already. They hear them at school or from playmates or read them in children's magazines. With a younger child, you can help him select something suitable. In guiding the child's choice of jokes or riddles, make sure it is something well within his vocabulary, containing only words and phrases with which he is already familiar, so that he can recite it fairly smoothly.

When you assemble in the living room, arrange it so that everyone is seated more or less in a straight line or in a slight semicircle. This is important, because they are going to be an audience, and they need to be in front of the speaker. No one should be seated behind the speaker or so far away that he can't make eye contact with them.

If you live in a small apartment and you don't have a family room, the kitchen or dining area will do nicely. Family members can sit on three sides of the table, and the speaker can stand on the end. Just be resourceful.

Since this is new to the children, you may want to explain a little more about what the meeting is about and give them an idea of what is expected of them. You might say:

> *We're going to have a Talk & Read Session. (For younger children you might add: It's something like Show & Tell at school.) We're going to start off with some riddles and jokes. I'll go first, so you can see how to do it.*

Then you rise, face the group, and say a riddle. Give the children time to guess the answers before going on to the next. Remember that even an old riddle can work as well as a new one. Don't hesitate to bring up one you remember from your own childhood. You might begin with this classic rhyming riddle:

> As I was going to St. Ives
> I met a man with seven wives;
> Every wife had seven sacks,
> Every sack had seven cats;
> Ever cat had seven kits:
> Kits, cats, sacks and wives,
> How many were going to St. Ives?

Here's some others:

> Riddle: What time is it when three hippos are in your bed?
> Answer: Time to get a new bed.

> Riddle: A man went to the store and bought the largest thing there. What was it?
> Answer: The store.

After you have told several riddles, then sit down and ask the children to

Chapter Nine: Riddles, Jokes & Silly Stories

take turns at it. The child should stand in front of the family. If he forgets, you can give him a friendly nudge, something like: "Let's see. You were going to tell the riddle about the clock, weren't you? And it seems to me it had something to do with telling time..."

At this point, he'll suddenly remember, and he's off and away. "Oh yeah. I remember now."

> Riddle: What time is it when the clock says thirty-four?
> Answer: Time to get a new clock.
>
> Riddle: What runs all the way around a yard but never moves?
> Answer: A fence.

Each child should do more than one riddle, so he gets practice speaking in front of everyone. After everyone has had a chance to tell some riddles, you can have some fun with tongue twisters. This is an impromptu (unprepared) exercise as far as the children are concerned.

It seems nonsensical on the surface, but there's a serious purpose to it. It will help everyone enunciate clearly, especially certain sounds which are formed at the front of the mouth.

For this exercise, everyone can remain seated except you. You're the guide this time. Say the tongue twister slowly, with some exaggeration. Then point to each child in turn, asking him to repeat it after you. Don't be too serious with this. Your first session is to be kept light and entertaining so that the children enjoy it. You don't want the children to feel embarrassed if they can't do if perfectly.

Begin with an easy tongue twister that even younger children can say, like the following:

> A big black bug bit a big black bear.

After each child has said it slowly, ask them to do it again, a little faster this time. Next, try one of these, which are a bit harder:

She sells seashells, shall he sell seashells?

Sally sells shiny seashells.

Take a ticket to Tacoma.

Tow a toy boat.

Rubber baby-buggy bumpers.

The following is an ancient one, which is a challenge for older children and adults as well. Slow down on this one. Take time to enunciate carefully the **sts** sound wherever it occurs.

Amidst the mists and coldest frosts,
With stoutest wrists and loudest boasts,
He thrusts his fists against the posts
And still insists he sees the ghosts.

Now take turns telling jokes. Again, each person should rise and face the group when it's his turn. Don't read the jokes. Tell them from memory, using your own words. Do the best you can, and encourage the children to do the same. Resources for jokes and riddles are included at the end of this chapter.

Here's some examples to get you started:

Mary: What was the reason you left your job?
Jimmy: Illness. The boss got sick of me.

Letter carrier: Is this package for you? The name is blurred.
Resident: No, it can't be mine. My name is Smith.

Customer: What is the price of that parrot?
Clerk: Five dollars.
Customer: OK, you can send me the bill.
Clerk: Sorry, but you have to take the whole bird.

If the child balks about taking part or is unprepared, don't attempt to force him to participate. Be casual, good-natured, and call on someone else and go on with the session. If the child feels that everyone who is participating is having a good time, he will probably be eager to join in next week.

Here's a good listening game. Explain that you are going to tell a story that everyone already knows. (It could be "The Three Bears" or "The Three Little Pigs" or something similar.) Say that you want to see how well everyone listens. You are going to tell the story, but with errors here and there. Each time you say something wrong, something that doesn't belong in the story, they should raise their hands to show that they caught the error.

Tell the story rather slowly. It could go something like this:

Once upon a time there were _four_ bears who lives in a house by the woods. (Hands should go up when you say _four_ instead of _three_.)

One morning when they were eating breakfast, they discovered that their _ice cream_ was too hot. Mama Bear said, "While we're waiting for it to cool down, let's go for a walk in the woods." So they all put on their _roller skates_ and went for a walk.

While they were gone, a little girl named _Raggedy Ann_ came by. She saw the door was open and she went in. She saw four chairs in the room. She sat down in the biggest chair and found it very _comfortable_.

She was hungry, and when she saw the bowls of ice cream on the table, she ate them all up.

Then she went upstairs, where she found _four little beds._ She was sleepy and she lay down on the big bed, but it was too hard. She tried the other beds, but they were too soft. _And so she lay down on the floor and went to sleep._

> Soon the bears came home. They discovered that someone had eaten their ice cream. The smallest bear said, "That's OK; I _don't like ice cream anyway._"
>
> But the father frowned. "Let's go look upstairs," he growled.
>
> When they went upstairs, the found that all the beds _looked neat,_ just as they had left them. But over in the corner, on the floor, they saw Raggedy Ann, asleep.
>
> She woke up, saw the bears, and was frightened. She rushed past them, went down the stairs, whizzed out of the house, and she _hopped and skipped all the way home._

If the children do a good job of listening and catching most of the errors, be sure to compliment them. You want to encourage them to be good listeners, not only in these sessions, but in school and elsewhere.

Here's another speech game you can play. It's appropriate for children ages 9 and older. It's an impromptu exercise and calls for active imagination.

You rise and begin telling a story, one that you are making up on the spot. Then, as you reach an exciting or suspenseful part, you break off and ask someone else to stand up and continue with the story, using their own imagination. Continue doing this until everyone has had a turn.

It could go something like this:

> Young Jimmy Jones was sitting alone at home one day. The rest of the family had gone out. The house was very quiet.
>
> All at once he heard a strange noise coming from another room. He wondered what it was and went to investigate. What could it be?
>
> The noise seemed to be coming from a closet in one of the bedrooms. He listened carefully. There it went again! It was a kind of low whirring sound ... very odd.
>
> The room was rather dark because the shades had been left down. Jimmy went over to the closet door and opened it. He was surprised to see ...

At this point you break off and let your spouse or one of the children take it from here. Give each child a little breathing space, a few second to get his thoughts together. Be sure that everyone understands how the game is played. Each one should push the story along a little bit, leaving it to the last person to provide the ending.

It need not be a realistic story. It can be as fanciful or as humorous as you wish. For instance, one might choose to place a comic strip character in the closet, or maybe an alien from outer space. Let each one make up a few lines on the spot, being creative. The more ridiculous the story becomes, the more fun it is.

This is an excellent way to stimulate a free flow of language. Since it is impromptu, it encourages each child to think on his feet.

It is not necessary to do all of the activities listed in this chapter on the same evening. You may save some ideas for another session, or incorporate ones from a following chapter. In fact, mixing and matching activities will encourage improvement of several types of skills, as you will see in the following chapters.

> **You'll know you've done a good job as a leader if, at the end of this first session you hear someone say, "That was fun! Can we do it again?"**

Resources for Riddles, Jokes, & Silly Stories

Use newspapers and the library often for Family Talk & Read sessions. Some ideas to get started are:

Cerf, Bennett. *Book of Animal Riddles.*

Cerf, Bennett. *Book of Laughs.*

Highlights for Children, a major national children's magazine. Address: PO Box 269, 2300 W 5th Ave., Columbus OH 43272-0002.

Reader's Digest, a major monthly magazine, contains regular features of jokes, riddles, and humorous anecdotes.

Chapter Ten: Reading Aloud

CHAPTER TEN:

FAMILY TALK & READ SESSION TWO
READING ALOUD

Purpose:

To help children appreciate reading
To improve oral reading
To gain confidence speaking in front of an audience
To improve the flow of language
Learning to transmit meaning through voice and manner

The next Family Talk & Read session can begin with some jokes and riddles again to create a lively atmosphere. Then some reading aloud should begin. This will mean there will need to be some preparation. Each child should be asked to bring something to read, whether it be a poem, his favorite book, or other reading material. You can help younger children decide what to bring.

Everyone can remain seated for this part of the program. The reader can sit on the sofa with others, or in a separate chair, whatever is most comfortable. You begin by choosing a story, a poem, or a chapter out of a children's novel. Again, you will be setting the proper mood and giving the children an idea of what is expected of them as participants.

Choose your selection carefully. Make sure it will hold the interest of the children. Consider their special interests carefully when selecting material. For this meeting, choose a book or story that is new to the children. Since the first read aloud session is preparing the way for those that follow, make a little extra effort to help it go right. Perhaps a colorfully illustrated book, one with lively, interesting characters, might be a good selection. It can be whimsical or not, but it should deal with things and ideas that children can understand and relate to—things from <u>their</u> world.

If you choose to read a poem, it should have strong rhyme and rhythm, since these elements appeal to most children. Avoid poems with a lot of abstract terms and symbolism. Children lack experience to interpret that type of poetry.

The mood of the selection can be serious, as in a mystery tale or a spooky story, but there should be plenty of action and suspense to hold their interest. If it's a story that's too long to finish in one evening, fine. Just stop in an exciting place, and say: "I can't finish the story tonight; it's too long. Besides, it's time to give someone else a turn to read." (And this technique may also give rise to a request for another session soon!)

There's a wealth of literature available for children, and resources are listed at the end of this chapter.

One suggestion for beginning is the all-time favorite poem, *Casey at the Bat* by Ernest Lawrence Thayer. Familiarize yourself with the poem by reading it over ahead of the meeting. Practice reading it <u>aloud</u> so that you'll do a more effective job when you read if for the family.

Read for your family rather slowly, so that your listeners can savor the full effect. Let them visualize Casey's proud scornful manner; let them hear his loyal supporters voicing their wrath at the umpire; and finally, let them feel the atmosphere of gloom when, incredibly, Casey strikes out.

Next, ask which child is ready to read his selection. A page or two is plenty for a younger child. It should be a suitable piece for him that is <u>easy to read</u>. It should have simple vocabulary which is familiar, and—most important—it should be something he <u>likes</u>. It might be a primer that he has mastered from school. Or it could be more fanciful, such as Dr. Seuss' *Cat in the Hat*.

Never mind if it's a book that has been around the house for ages, even a favorite one that he's read over and over. In fact, that's exactly what you want, for your child to read something he really enjoys and has mastered. What you <u>don't</u> want is for him to try to read from a book he's never seen before, because it will present problems in word recognition. If he plods along slowly, having to stop frequently to ask the meaning of this word and that, then the purpose of the session is defeated. This is not meant to be a reading lesson: that would bore the rest of the family and derail the meeting.

Remember, the purpose of this session is not to teach your child how to read, but rather to help him read <u>aloud</u>, to express himself orally. In both speaking and oral reading, there has to be a flow of language. The words are already known but the speaker has to learn how to release them in a controlled, effective way. Your child understands the words—the thoughts, ideas and emotions they convey—but he has yet to learn how to transmit that meaning to others through his voice and manner.

Whatever your child reads and however it goes, say something good about his performance. No criticism. Later you can give pointers about how to improve oral presentation, but for now you should try to boost his confidence.

Perhaps your 9-year-old child has brought home a book from the library about space adventure. He plans to read aloud a chapter to the family. Encourage him to read it over to himself first, preferably aloud. If convenient, he should practice reading it for one parent. This "rehearsal" should precede family reading sessions after the first read-aloud session.

Reading aloud is different from reading silently. It calls into play different abilities and techniques. It's never safe to assume that because you can read something silently that you can do a good job of reading it aloud to an audience. Lack of preparation invariably leads to poor performance.

Everyone should have a chance to read aloud. Younger children should read a page or two; middle grade children can read a short chapter; older children may want to read a longer chapter or longer poems.

Try to build a warm, friendly atmosphere. Offer no direct criticism of your children's performance at this time. Think of yourself not as a teacher at this point, but as a guide on a family excursion. Each of you is there to learn something; but in addition, you're there to enjoy being together and to share a pleasant experience. Relax and take things as they come.

After everyone has a chance to read aloud, take a few minutes to read together. Have photocopies of a poem prepared for this. Select material that is rather catchy and fun. Say something like, "We're going to read this poem together. If some of the words are too hard for you younger readers, just skip over them for now and try to follow along as much as possible." Two people can share each copy, with the older one moving over the words with his fingers so that the younger one can follow along, even if he doesn't know all the words.

The reading aloud part of Family Talk & Read sessions is very important, and should generally be included each week, possibly with other activities such as the family discussion, explained in the next chapter.

Resources for Reading Aloud

Young children (ages 7-9):
The Swing a poem by Robert Lewis Stevenson.
My Shadow a poem by Robert Lewis Stevenson.
A Child's Garden of Verses a book of poetry by Robert Lewis Stevenson. Watts 1966.
The Tale of Peter Rabbit by Beatrix Potter. Warne, 1902.
Henry Huggins by Beverly Cleary. Morrow 1950.
Ramona Quimby and other Ramona books by Beverly Cleary.
Winnie the Pooh by A. A. Milne. Dutton 1926.

Middle-grade children (ages 10-12)

A Child's Garden of Verses a book of poetry by Robert Lewis Stevenson.

The Owl & The Pussycat, a poem by Edward Lear.

Alice in Wonderland by Lewis Carroll. Large type with colorful pictures edition available from Western Publishing Company, 1976.

James & The Giant Peach by Ronald Dahl. Published by Knopf, 1961 and Bantam, 1978.

Charlotte's Web by E. B. White. Harper, 1952.

Little House on the Prairie and the entire "Little House" series by Laura Ingalls Wilder. Harper 1953.

Island of the Blue Dolphins by Scott O'Dell. Houghton Mifflin 1960.

Julie of the Wolves by Jean George. Harper, 1972.

Anne Frank: The Diary of a Young Girl by Anne Frank. Doubleday 1967.

Golden Treasure of Poetry Louis Untermeyer. Western 1959.

The Voyages of Dr. Doolittle by Hugh Lofting. Lippincott.

Older children (ages 13+)

The Sea Chest by Captain Frank Knight. Platt & Munk Company, 1964.

A Wrinkle in Time by Madeleine L'Engle. Farrar, 1962.

Little Women by Louisa May Alcott. Dutton, 1948.

The Adventures of Tom Sawyer by Mark Twain. Macmillan, 1966.

Anthologies of Children's Literature

The Illustrated Treasury of Children's Literature edited by Margaret E. Martignoni.Published by Grosset & Dunlap, 1955.

Guides to Children's Literature

Cline, Ruth & William McBride. *A Guide to Literature for Young Adults: Background, Selection & Use.* Scott, Foresman & Company, 1983.

Lukens, Rebecca J. *A Critical Handbook of Children's Literature.* Scott, Foresman & Company, 1982. Includes lists of award-winning literature.

90 **Dorothy Hamill**

"CHAMPION ON ICE"
DOROTHY HAMILL

The following is a reading selection from the book *They Reached For The Stars* by Ruth Turk. This book contains 12 profiles of celebrities and sport figures who have overcome great difficulties to achieve tremendous goals. This book will motivate and inspire young readers. It is available from Blue Bird Publishing. Order form on page 128.

The ice skates were too big for the little girl but her grandmother made them fit by padding them with foam rubber. Though she was only 8-years-old, Dorothy Hamill couldn't wait to get on the ice. Her fingers were freezing cold, but she laced the boots herself. At last she stood up, hobbling a little bit. Then she took a deep breath and began to move out. The moment she felt the smooth hard surface under her blades, a warm rush of excitement surged through her body.

The small girl grew up to win the title of World Figure Skating Champion but there was never a time she failed to get that feeling of excitement when she was on the ice. Her first pair of skates had been in the family for some time. They had been used by her brother, Sandy, and her sister, Marcia, but it didn't matter as long as she could use them, too. One of the reasons she loved visiting her grandparents who lived in the next town was that there was a large pond right behind their house. During the winter when Morse's Pond froze solid, Dorothy would skate back and forth for hours while her grandmother watched from the kitchen window.

"When I was shaking with cold I'd rush into the house and let her rub my feet with a warm bath towel," Dorothy said. "Then she would give me a cup of steaming coffee laced heavily with sugar and real cream. Since my mother didn't allow us to have coffee, I never told her about it. Grandmother said it was good for me—the sugar would give me energy and the cream would give me calcium for my bones. 'If you're going to skate,' she told me, 'you have to make sure your bones are strong. Otherwise they'll break.' "

Dorothy listened to her grandmother, not only because she loved her, but also because she also didn't want anything to prevent her from skating. She couldn't wait until she owned her own ice skates. One day in the window of the local department store Dorothy spotted the most beautiful ice skates she had ever seen. They were white with bright red trim. When Mrs. Hamill heard how much they cost she shook her head.

"Maybe next Christmas," she said. Dorothy felt miserable. She realized there were more important things her parents needed to buy for a family of three children, but she wished it weren't so. She tried not to think about the wonderful skates in the window, but they danced in her dreams almost every night. One day she come home from school, and there, on the kitchen table, stood a large white box with her name on it. Mrs. Hamill smiled and pushed the box toward her wide-eyed daughter.

> "Since they mean so much to you, we thought you'd better have them," she said.

Dorothy opened the box. Inside, nestled in a bed of white tissue, were the most beautiful skates in the world. At last she had her very own pair, and they fit her perfectly. From that time on, Dorothy Hamill spent as much time as possible on the ice. At first the new skates felt terrific, and she loved gliding forward, moving a little faster as she gained more and more confidence.

There was one problem, though. There were a lot of other kids on the ice, and they skated forward <u>and</u> backwards. Not wanting to be left out, Dorothy tried to imitate them, but it didn't work. The moment she turned, she lost control of her legs and fell down. She got up and tried again and again, but she kept falling until she was so sore and bruised she went home in tears.

When Mrs. Hamill learned what happened, she enrolled her daughter for weekly lessons after school at an ice rink. Soon Dorothy learned to do the "Mohawk"— turning from a forward skating position to a backward position. She didn't realize it then, but the Mohawk is the first step toward competitive ice skating. When the first series of lessons was over, Dorothy wanted to learn more. During the summer when it wasn't possible to skate outdoors in Connecticut, she went to an ice skating rink to continue her lessons. As her skating improved, Dorothy's enthusiasm grew. It was also hard work.

Before long, Dorothy was practicing seven hours a day, getting up at dawn to put in time before school, and continuing when she got home in the afternoon. At the Crystal Ice Palace in Norwalk, Connecticut, her instructor was Otto Gold, one of the country's most famous skating teachers. Mr. Gold was a strict disciplinarian, and at first, Dorothy was a little afraid of him. However, under his supervision, she learned the kinds of skating figures that emphasize the technique upon which all ice skating is based.

After a few months, Dorothy was ready to try out for her figure skating tests. These are a series of tests that establish the level of competence of individual skaters. They are administered under strict conditions in a registered skating club and are governed by the rules of the United States Figure Skating Association (U.S.F.S.A.). The first test is the Preliminary, followed by eight more. Skaters who pass the Eighth Test (or Gold Test) are qualified to compete in senior competitions. Since the headquarters of the Southern Connecticut Ice Skating Club were in the Crystal Ice Palace, it was a natural for Dorothy to try out.

In the spring, she took the preliminary test. Mrs. Gold helped Dorothy's mother sew a special dress for the event. Made of blue flannel, it swirled gracefully around Dorothy's slender thighs. The young skater was so proud of her new dress that she forgot to be nervous.

When Dorothy passed her test, Mr. Gold invited her to come to Lake Placid to train with him during the summer. Lake Placid, in the Adirondack Mountains of New York State, is one of the great sports capitals of the world and an important summer training center for competition skaters. Dorothy was thrilled that her teacher thought she was good enough, but would her parents allow her to go? When Mr. Gold said that Dorothy could live with his family and take daily lessons, her parents agreed to let the 9-year-old spend her first summer away from home.

It was not easy for Dorothy to say good-bye to her friends, especially Kim, a girl her age with whom she was very close.

During the weeks that followed, Dorothy missed her friend and her family, but skating started to take over her life more and more. There was no time to be homesick because Mr. Gold worked his students hard. Even when she became

Dorothy Hamill

exhausted from so many hours on the ice, Dorothy felt a growing sense of exhilaration because she was learning so much.

In July of that year, Dorothy turned 10 and passed her first figure test. Two weeks later she passed her second test. In between practice, she watched the great skating champions on the rink as they prepared for the big Lake Placid exhibition. She wondered if someday she would skate like them. Only time would tell—time, constant hard work, and giving up some of the things most girls enjoy having when they are in their teens.

As Dorothy's techniques improved with daily practice, other things suffered. On her return home, the Hamill household had to be arranged around her schedules. She and her sister Marcia started fighting over their room, their clothes, and the sharing of chores. Since brother Sandy was the oldest and planning on going to school out of town, he stayed out of the conflicts between his sisters. Sometimes Dorothy longed for the days when she was seven or eight and Sandy used to play chess with her, but there wasn't time for such things anymore. She missed him when he left but there was a compensating factor. Instead of having to share a room with her sister, now she had a room of her own.

Dorothy continued to pass her skating tests and though she was proud of these accomplishments, her school work began to deteriorate. She would arrive in class so tired from early morning workouts that she had difficulty staying awake.

She looked forward to summer when she could return to Lake Placid and would not have to worry about regular classes. She was in her element at Lake Placid. It was there that she entered free skating competitions and did so well that her teacher said she might qualify for the National Competitions. Dorothy also began to study with

Sonya Dunfield, a former National Champion and Olympic competitor.

Once during the Christmas vacation she met a boy named David. He was serving refreshments at the stand next to the ice rink. Dorothy thought David had the bluest eyes she had ever seen. At the end of the week, he called to ask her to go out with him on New Year's Eve. This was the first time anyone had asked Dorothy for a date and she was excited. At the Lake Placid Country Club, the young ice skater had a wonderful New Year's Eve, but it was over all too soon. She had to be home by midnight because she had to be up early New Year's Day to practice. The National Championships were only a few weeks away.

Dorothy's mother took her to Manhattan where a French dressmaker designed a special costume for her to wear in the Nationals. It was made of pale-green, sequined material that shimmered like magic. It was the first costume of its kind she had ever owned. Dorothy couldn't wait to wear it.

On the morning of the big event, Dorothy woke up feeling not exactly sick, but strange. Her father felt her forehead but it wasn't hot. Her teacher told her to take deep breaths and relax.

"You'll be just fine once you get going," she said. Dorothy didn't know what was wrong. She took deep breaths. She wanted to make her parents proud of her. She looked down at the beautiful green dress that sparkled in the light.

"I can't do this," Dorothy said. "I can't go out there and skate."

The prospect of performing before thousands of people had given Dorothy Hamill her first case of stage fright. As she heard her name over the loudspeakers and people starting to applaud, the young girl thought her heart would stop beating. Her skin broke out in goosebumps. But Sonya Dunfield put her hand gently on her pupil's shoulder.

"You can't quit now, Dorothy," she said. " Just forget everything except the ice."

And that's what happened. Dorothy moved out on the smooth icy surface in time to the music. Suddenly, a hush fell over the audience. The skater in the green dress felt the energy flood her body and knew she was going to be all right. All the fear and panic melted away and she swirled and floated like a swan on home territory. At the end, Dorothy landed in a double toe loop jump and finished with a flourish before the judges' stand. When she came off the ice, she saw her teacher smiling at her.

"You did well," she said, hugging the young skater. "I'm proud of you."

Dorothy's father came rushing toward his daughter and lifted her in the air. "You did it!" he shouted. "You won the Novice Champion!"

It was true. Teenager Dorothy Hamill had won a National Figure Skating Championship. From that time on, Dorothy scarcely had time for school studies, romance, or anything but competitive figure ice-skating.

In seventh grade, her mother encouraged Dorothy to attend the spring dance, but said she would have to be home by eight o'clock. That was an hour extension on her normal bedtime when she was preparing for a skating competition. The night of the dance Mr. Hamill drove his daughter to the school. She went into the hall and realized she was the first one there. Gradually people began to arrive. Dorothy looked around hoping that a certain boy on whom she had a crush would also come early. As

Dorothy Hamill

the hands of the clock crept toward eight, Dorothy started to give up hope. A moment later the boy came through the door, but so did Dorothy's father. Mr. Hamill looked at Dorothy.

Dorothy looked at the boy, but it was too late. He never saw her. Dorothy went home with her father and cried herself to sleep.

When Dorothy was 14, she was given permission to leave school so she could train and compete without interruption. In her hours off the ice, she studied with a private tutor and completed her education. Her parents traveled with her whenever possible, but she seldom got to see her brother and sister when she was in training away from home.

When Dorothy went to Denver, Colorado, to train with Carlo Fassi, who was considered the best figure skating coach in the world, she was in the company of 30 other skaters, foreign as well as American, who were studying with him. Now the competition was getting tougher. Sometimes Dorothy got mad at herself for not doing better. Many champions have an enormous amount of confidence in themselves, but this was not true of Dorothy. It worried Mr. Fassi.

"If you want to convince the judges that you're the best, you must first convince yourself," he told his young pupil.

Gradually, the skating coach taught Dorothy to relax more and carefully polish her skating style. In order to enter the Olympics she would have to be ready to compete against the world's finest stylists. In February 1976, Dorothy Hamill arrived in the old city of Innsbruck, Austria, along with cross-country skiers, ski racers, bobsledders, figure skaters, TV crews, and reporters from every corner of the globe. Many spectators who had come to watch the proceedings were anxious for Dorothy to win in the Olympics. Some of them had watched her at home and were charmed by her radiant smile and graceful skating. It had taken Dorothy many years of intensive practice to execute the intricate leaps and figures she knew so well.

Then an unfortunate thing happened. In her final warm-up, Dorothy had a fall. She insisted on getting up, but she felt sore and shaky. Meanwhile, she could hear the applause for the other performers coming from the arena. Her coach and her parents watched Dorothy anxiously, but she stood up quickly, even though inwardly she was trembling.

Now it was her turn. As Dorothy's name was announced, she straightened her shoulders and pushed off onto the ice. The crowds began to cheer and call her name. As the music for Dorothy's routine floated on the air, she moved around the huge rink with the graceful, flowing movements and intricate turns the American skater had become known for.

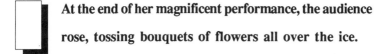

At the end of her magnificent performance, the audience rose, tossing bouquets of flowers all over the ice.

After the rink was cleared, several other performers went through their paces, but when the scores were in, Dorothy Hamill had won the gold medal for figure skating in the 1976 Olympic competitions.

The American public was very proud of Dorothy. When she returned to the United States, she was greeted with cheers and applause wherever she went. The National Women's Republican Club awarded her the Outstanding Young Woman of the Year Award. At home in Connecticut, people turned out to watch their heroine ride through the streets in a triumphal motorcade. When the motorcade stopped at the pond where Dorothy first learned to skate, a plaque was dedicated to her. The Olympic champion was thrilled by her popularity, especially when she received tons of fan mail. Soon girls all over the country rushed to get their hair cut "Dorothy Hamill Style."

Through all the excitement and honors, Dorothy never lost a sense of humility and wonder that all this was happening to her. Her Olympic victory brought with it opportunities she had never dreamed possible. She was wined, dined, driven in stretch limousines and bombarded with flowers and compliments. She was signed for TV commercials and TV specials. Things became so complicated it was necessary to hire a manager to help determine the direction of Dorothy's career.

For the next three years the former Olympic champ became the star of the popular ice show, *Ice Capades*. She appeared in cities all over the country, winning new fans wherever she went. In Los Angeles, one of her most ardent fans was a young actor named Dean Martin, Jr. In 1982, Dorothy and Dean were married in a beautiful ceremony in Beverly Hills. Since then, one of the accomplishments of which the star is justly proud is her ice-skating clinics for handicapped kids.

"I want to let these special children know how important they are and to share with them some of the good fortune I have had in my own life," Dorothy said.

"When I watch them struggling to achieve goals they have set for themselves—small goals for others, giant goals for them—I am always overwhelmed by their courage. When I leave them, I take away with me a resumed sense of hope and belief in the essential value of life."

 It is quite obvious that Dorothy Hamill is not only one of the greatest skaters in the world, but also a genuine champion in the most important sense of the word.

CHAPTER ELEVEN:

FAMILY TALK & READ SESSION THREE
FAMILY DISCUSSION

<u>**Purpose:**</u>

Stimulate creative thinking
Encourage analytical thought
Develop moral character and values
Encourage the expression of opinions
Improve oral presentation

Another type of activity that you can bring into Family Talk & Read sessions is a family discussion. This adds variety to the type of speaking that the child is encouraged to develop. Perhaps every third or fourth session could be reserved strictly for a family discussion. Regardless of the topic, the evening will be a speech exercise for everyone.

There is no limit to possible suitable topics. The choice is best left up to you. Keep in mind that whatever you choose to discuss, it must be something within the range of the children's experience and understanding.

Avoid abstract topics, especially for younger children, and select ones that are down-to-earth and deal with concrete concepts. It could be something related to home, family, school, relatives, neighbors, or community happenings. Some topics are too broad and should be narrowed down. Occasionally you can let the topic be chosen by the children.

This activity has a special benefit of being a good time for character-building and is an opportunity to help children establish high moral values.

For example, you could start off the discussion by telling the legend about the "boy who cried wolf." Then bring the example closer to home and ask questions such as: Do you know someone who fibs? Do you admire him? Why does he do this?

You might choose to tackle and perhaps revolve certain family problems that have arisen: division of household chores; sibling rivalry; or allowances.

For this type of activity, everyone can remain seated. There are a few point to keep in mind so that everything will go smoothly. Let the children know the topic in advance of the meeting. Urge them to think about it and be ready to contribute opinions and ideas.

At the meeting, introduce the topic, making it clear to everyone, and identifying the problem (if there is one) to be resolved. Explain that it is necessary to take turns speaking and that it will be considered rude to interrupt others. Encourage each child to speak clearly. Get them to stick to the point.

Teach your children that they should not remain silent when they have something worthwhile to say. Encourage them to express themselves by asking sensible questions, voicing opinions, and actively contributing to the discussion. You can draw them into the discussion by saying, "Susan, what do you think about that?"

On the other hand, don't let one child monopolize the discussion. And if one child should disagree with another, he should do so without making disparaging personal remarks. Emphasize the important of being polite when expressing a difference of opinion.

Try to see that a shy younger child is not overwhelmed by an older brother or sister. See that all have a chance to take part.

Stay flexible and keep your sense of humor. It is not always necessary to reach a consensus or solve a problem under consideration. Suppose that the discussion involved where the family should go for summer vacation. Everyone might have a different idea and no agreement could be reached. You can close the discussion by saying: "Well, we've heard some good suggestions. Of course, we don't need to decide this right now. We can think about it some more in the weeks ahead, and make a decision later on."

It's a good idea to make the family discussion one part of a Talk & Read session, and to save time for oral reading. The combination of activities helps develop several skills.

CHAPTER TWELVE:

HELPING CHILDREN IMPROVE IN ORAL COMMUNICATION

This chapter is an explanation of the techniques that a parent can use to help his children improve their speech and reading aloud. Using these methods during Family Talk & Read sessions will be very effective.

This program of Family Talk & Read sessions will help your children learn mostly by doing. It is important to build a warm, receptive atmosphere for them to practice in, and there should be little or no direct criticism of their efforts.

Later on, when they have the chance to participate in an oral activity at school or in church, they will be enthusiastic and eager to take part. Their response will be, "Oh sure. I can do that! I've done it lots of times before."

<u>Be Generous With Praise</u>

Be generous with your praise. It will give them self confidence and a positive feeling about speaking and expressing themselves.

When the child finished his talk and sits down, you should compliment him. Look for something you can sincerely praise, such as clear speech or good posture. "I like the way you stood up so nice and straight while you were speaking." "That was fine, Jeff. You spoke clearly and I could understand every word you said." "You made fine eye contact."

You can always comment on the subject itself in a positive cheerful way. If he spoke about how much fun it was to go on a picnic, you can say, "I've always enjoyed picnics too!"

Maintain good rapport!

Once your family is well launched on this program of weekly sessions you can give them specific bits of advice on ways to improve their speech. The following is suggestions based on the children's ages.

How to Improve Speech & Oral Reading in Young Children Ages 6-7

Experts who have worked with children in elementary school advise not to call attention to the speaking process itself with younger children, ages 6 and 7. Let their speaking flow naturally from subjects they are interested in, and don't talk to them about specific techniques of delivery. At this age, the most important thing is to make sure that his participation in family reading sessions is a pleasant, enjoyable experience. Show an interest in what he is saying.

Let the younger child choose his own subjects for the family sessions. The subject should spring from his own experience. If he appears uncertain, then give him some suggestions. For him, the session can be much like Show & Tell at school. He may want to bring an item to show and talk about—perhaps a bird's feather he found, or a pretty rock, or a picture he cut out of a magazine. He can hold it up and tell about it: where it came from, and why he likes it.

Children of this age do not organize the material in their talks as older people do. But they can stick to the point, and they are aware of some of the basic orders of speech, such as: first, second, third; middle and end; earlier and later; etc. With the help of an adult they can make lists of things.

You can encourage this orderly way of thinking by asking the child questions in advance of his talk. Suppose he's going to tell about the time he stayed with

Chapter Twelve: Helping Children Improve In Oral Communication

his grandparents on the farm. Ask him, "What different animals did you see?" (You can help him list them.) "I saw horses, and cows, and chickens and ducks ... But I liked their dog, Ruffy, best of all."

Help him describe things, using words such as: big and little; tall and short; up and down; in and out; over and under. Encourage a child of this age to use complete sentences. When you ask him questions, avoid the kind that can be answered with a simple yes or no. Instead of asking, "Did you like the farm?" you should ask, "How did you like the farm?"

> **When the child is giving his talk, avoid interrupting him. You want to encourage a smooth, unself-conscious flow of language.**

If the child is not speaking distinctly, don't call attention to this directly, especially while the child is giving his talk. He is trying to remember his train of thought, and if he is made to think of how he sounds, he will be distracted, and your whole purpose will be defeated.

Instead, try speech games with tongue twisters. In family discussions you can emphasize the importance of clear speech in various ways. You can mention how on the telephone certains words that sound similar can easily be misunderstood. Words like sun and fun; man and ran; fell and tell, bake and take; we and me. Tell why people need to make more of an effort to open their mouths when their speak, using their lips and tongue to make certain sounds, especially beginning sounds on the front of words (consonants like b, p, f, and t).

Children in this youngest age group are also losing baby teeth and gaining permanent teeth. If the two front teeth are missing, the child will have difficulty speaking clearly. This is another reason we should encourage him to speak but not directly call attention to his mistakes. Be sure that the older children do not tease or belittle the younger ones.

How to Improve Speech & Oral Reading in Children Ages 8-9

Children ages 8 and 9 are becoming a little more aware of speech as a tool. They are beginning to use the dictionary to look up words and they add these words to their speaking vocabulary. They are learning to use discussion as a means of solving problems. They use the telephone for sending and receiving messages. You can teach children this age not only <u>what</u> to say but <u>how</u> to say it, on a basic level.

<u>Telephone manners:</u>

These children can be taught telephone manners. Explain that everyone should answer the phone in a polite, courteous way. They should also know the proper way to record a message: "He's not here right now. May I take a message?" Teach him to repeat the caller's phone number and the spelling of the caller's name.

Emphasize to these children that they should never give out certain information to strangers over the phone, such as, "There's nobody home except me." They should also be taught to limit their phone calls with their friends. Five minutes is a good limit.

<u>Vocabulary Building:</u>

If a child this age uses a word incorrectly or mispronounces a word during his talks, you might unobtrusively jot the word down in your notebook and tell him about it later. Consult the dictionary together—not only to solve the immediate problems, but also to get him into the habit of using a dictionary.

To help him learn the correct meaning of the word: <u>say</u> the word, <u>write</u> it down, and <u>show</u> it to him. Then use it in a sentence and ask him to repeat the sentence after you. This way he's more likely to remember it.

Mention the importance of using words accurately. Tell him to use the right word in the right place. Explain that words showing strong or intense emotion should be used in moderation. For example, he should not use the word "hate" if he means "dislike." Hate conveys a stronger emotion and should not be used carelessly or frequently.

Encourage Organization

Children this age can indicate at the beginning of their talks what main points they intend to cover. Encourage some organization in their remarks. You can do this best by talking it over with the child ahead of the family session. For example, if he has chosen the topic of a trip to the zoo, you can suggest that he narrow it down to the two or three sights he enjoyed the most. Perhaps it was the giraffes or the elephants. That would be his main points. He can give some details about each one. This kind of planning helps him think clearly and stick to the point.

Some children have difficulty sticking to the subject. They tend to ramble and talk too long. They need to be reminded to stick to the point, and when they are through, to sit down. If your child has this tendency, remind him of it before he speaks. Help him pick a topic that is not too broad in scope, and settle on a few specific things to say about it. Urge him to think about this in advance.

Hints on Speech Delivery

1. Eye contact. If necessary, remind him just before he gets up to speak, "Be sure and look at us while you're talking to us. Don't look out the window or down at the floor." Make sure you use good eye contact since you the the role model. You can explain why eye contact is important: "People like for you to look them in the eye when you speak to them. If you don't do it, they get bored and they stop listening to you. Then they start thinking about something else."

2. Smile. Advise your child to smile when he first gets up to speak. "This lets the audience know that you like them. Then they decide they like you and that they want to hear what you have to say." Explain this applies in school when giving an oral report, and also during an oral program.

3. Clear enunciation. To dramatize the importance of speaking clearly, you can deliberately mumble and slur your words so that no one can understand you. Your children will giggle over this, but you will get the point across. You might even invent a character such a "Molly Mumble" and say, "Don't be a Molly Mumble!" (or Frozen Face Freddy or Lazy Lips Larry). With a little exaggeration, show what happens when a person doesn't open his mouth sufficiently to speak or read aloud. Nearly-closed lips and a lazy tongue make it hard for listeners to understand what is said.

4. Speak up. If a child tends to speak too softly or uses a breathy tone, try this. Pretend you are a deaf old man. Go stand in the doorway or in the hall, so that you are a little distance away from the rest of the family. Then ask each child in turn to say a designated sentence as loudly and clearly as possible. The sentence could be, "Are you going to the store?" Explain to the children that shouting doesn't count. Each one should try to speak twice as loud as he does ordinarily. Remind them that increased volume alone isn't enough. They must speak clearly, using lips, teeth and tongue to get the message across.

5. Rate of speech. The older the child, the more he should be encouraged to speak fairly rapidly, if possible. This keeps the thoughts and ideas flowing at a moderately rapid rate. Most above-average speakers have this characteristic in common. Good salesmen, top-notch business executives, and successful administrators usually speak rapidly. Speech researchers have found that we think four times faster than we speak. This means if we are listening to a slow speaker, there's a great time lag in our brain. That's why our mind tends to wander. A rapid speaker, whoever, tends to take up this slack and succeeds in holding the listeners' attention.

6. Pauses. Used effectively, pauses can enhance a speech. Good speakers make use of them frequently. A speaker might pause after making a startling statement. He wants to make sure the audience takes it in and has time to think about it. A pause is also a good transition device. Pausing might indicate, "Now we're moving on to something else." When used properly, pauses indicate that the speaker is poised and in control of himself.

7. "and-uh." This meaningless expression comes across as a minor annoyance which tends to get in the listener's way. It occurs frequently in ordinary everyday conversation, but we tend to overlook it. When giving a talk, the speaker should try to hold the number of "and-uhs" to a minimum. But don't feel that just because they creep in now and then that an otherwise good speech is a total failure.

8. Inflection, expression, and emphasis. A pause in the right place or a change in rate or volume can add emphasis and meaning to oral reading. The children will learn these techniques mostly by watching you. If you read with expression, they will tend to do so also. You will notice that they will adopt your interpretations and will mirror your delivery, tone for tone, phrase for phrase. Demonstrate emphasis by using a little more force and a rising pitch on key words.

Examples: He was surprised to look down and see a teeny-tiny man looking up at him.

        Guess what I got for Christmas? A BRAND-NEW BICYCLE!

        To dance the waltz, you must count: ONE, two three; ONE two three.

        Boy: I lost the $50 you gave me. Dad: You did WHAT?

9. Phrasing. Explain that proper phrasing of oral reading helps listeners understand the meaning of the material. You group together words that carry a single thought or idea. Present ideas and thoughts one at a time, using slight pauses between, giving proper emphasis to key words. Punctuation, such as commas, can be an aid in phrasing, but you cannot depend on it. Rely instead on the meaning of the words. Phrase accordingly. Break down long or involved sentences into smaller, easily understood units.

10. Voice quality and tone. The children are probably already aware that there are pleasant voices, ugly voices, smooth voices, rasping voices, and nasal voices. Talk about the effect of a pleasant-sounding voice. We all like to hear a warm, cheerful voice that has a lilt in it. Cheerfulness is catching. Point out that whining is a bad habit. Children can also learn how to change their voices to match the part of the characters that are supposed to be speaking. This will be a lot of fun. For example, in the story "The Three Little Pigs," they need to distinguish the voice of the wolf from those of the

pigs. The wolf's voice can be strong and gruff, while those of the pigs would be pitched slightly higher and sound rather timid and fearful.

How to Improve Speech in Older Children Ages 10-12

Older children are much more sophisticated about the uses of speech. They may be called upon to look up information on a certain subject, organize it, and present it as an oral report in class. They take part in discussions, elect class officers and conduct meetings. You can discuss with this age child the how and why of speech and also give him helpful tips to improve his delivery.

They can go beyond their own experience when choosing a topic. It can be something they read or studied about. They can look up information in various reference books, or interview someone to gain facts. They can jot down this information and arrange it in an orderly, logical fashion.

These children are already aware that a speech has three parts: introduction, body, and conclusion. They can build a simple outline by noting the main points and sub-points for the body of their speech.

Attention-Getting Device

Emphasize the importance of a good introduction. It should be more than a mere announcement of the topic. It should begin with some attention-getting device. If the speaker does not succeed in getting the attention of the audience in the first few seconds of his speech, he probably won't get it at all.

Explain it to him this way: Imagine that your audience is getting sleepy, even before you get up to speak. You have to think of some way to rouse them and grab their attention. It isn't fair to clap your hands, to yell, or to set off a firecracker. So what can you do?

One way is to hold up an interesting object (visual aid) to stir their curiosity. A child telling about a camping experience could start out by showing an object he made in camp crafts class.

Another way to gain attention is to ask a question. For a talk about fire

**Chapter Twelve: Helping Children Improve
In Oral Communication**

safety: "What would you do if your house caught fire?" This is called a rhetorical question. Though the speaker asks a question, he doesn't expect the audience to reply. He merely wants them to think about it and consider it silently.

A story or a joke is another attention-getting device. It's important that this story or joke has some connection with the material to follow.

Types of Speeches

Older children are ready to learn that speeches have different purposes, and that speech preparation should keep in mind its purpose.

1. Informative speech. The speaker wants to explain something, to teach something new. Examples: "How to Refinish Furniture" or "My Trip to Africa." Your children will usually give this type of speech. They will be telling, explaining, or describing something that lies within their experience.

2. Persuasive speech. The speaker wants to convince someone of something, usually trying to get them to take a specific action. Example: salesman wanting to sell product or service.

3. Speech to impress. The speaker wants to leave a specific feeling. Example: a speech extolling patriotism.

4. Entertaining speech. The speaker want to provide humor or entertainment only.

Job Interviews

Older children will probably want some part-time work. You can help him by discussing some important aspects of interviews. Tell him how to prepare for them and what to expect. You can even rehearse the scene with him, pretending that you are the prospective employer. Going over it ahead of time will give him confidence.

Remind him that it's important to look neat and clean and to wear clothing that is appropriate for the job. Tell him to smile and to speak confidently. He should look ready to work and show a willingness to work. His voice should reflect enthusiasm.

He should be prepared to answer questions about his background and experience. When the job has been explained to him, he should indicate that he understands. When the interview is finished, he should thank the person and leave promptly.

Rules to Teach Children About Conversation

1. Be a good listener. Don't insist on doing all the talking.
2. Don't interrupt the other person.
3. Show an interest in what the person is saying.
4. Avoid arguing.
5. Be tactful. Don't bluntly contradict the other person.
6. If you find that you disagree with something and you feel you must say so, try to do it in a way that doesn't arouse resentment.
7. Don't talk about yourself constantly.
8. Don't ask questions or make comments that are too personal. Example: "How long have you had that pimple on your face?" "You're awfully short for your age."
9. Try to like others. Smile and be pleasant. Don't decide to dislike a newcomer before you have even spoken to him. You might miss the chance to know a very nice person.
10. Don't gossip. Don't speak critically of someone who is absent. Nearly always he will find out what you said anyway!
11. Be loyal to family and friends. Don't discuss private matters with outsiders.
12. When you are introduced to someone knew, try hard to remember their name. Use it during your conversation, try to fix it in your mind, and remember it the next time you meet.
13. When you're talking to a friend in a room filled with people, talk in a moderate or quiet tone. Don't be boisterous or noisy or attract attention to yourself.
14. Use good language. Avoid vulgar words. Habitual use of profanity indicates a poverty of expression.

Chapter Twelve: Helping Children Improve In Oral Communication

INDEX

MORE BOOKS
AVAILABLE FROM BLUE BIRD PUBLISHING
ORDER FORM ON PAGE 128

CHILDREN'S FICTION

SPACEDOG'S   BEST   FRIEND
By Toni Sweeney

Maybe   a   vacation...
Maybe   an   adventure...
Probably   the   most   important

summer   of   her   life!

Jenny's uncle offers her absolutely anything she wants for graduation. Her request: a space cruise! The cruise ends up being more than just a vacation when the spaceliner hits an asteroid cluster, and Jenny is spun into dark outer space in a lifepod—along with <u>three dogs</u>. These dogs are not ordinary dogs—<u>they talk</u>! (For children ages 9-15.)

TRULY A MODERN-DAY SWISS FAMILY ROBINSON!
ISBN 0-933025-13-0   208 pages, illustrated $6.95

OTHER TITLES

WHO'S WHO IN ANTIQUES (First Edition) by Cheryl Gorder is the only national comprehensive directory of the antique profession! Includes auction companies, show promoters, dealers, mall dealers, periodicals, appraisers, authors, services, and organizations.
ISBN 0-933025-02-5 $14.95

REAL DAKOTA: About Dakota by Dakotans, edited by Cheryl Gorder is a book that celebrates the Dakota Centennial in a very special way—it focuses on the people themselves. It a a unique book about Dakotans by Dakotans themselves.
ISBN 0-933025-07-6 $11.95

MORE PARENTING BOOKS
AVAILABLE FROM BLUE BIRD PUBLISHING
ORDER FORM ON PAGE 128

SCIENCE EDUCATION

SHARING NATURE WITH CHILDREN by Joseph Cornell. A Parents' and Teachers' Nature-Awareness Guidebook. Contains 42 nature-awareness games and activities that require no special education or expensive equipment. Perfect for home schoolers and other parents. This book has been adopted by the Girl Scouts and the Boy Scouts and has been endorsed by the National Audubon Society. It is used by parents, teachers, environmentalists, youth group leaders, and camp directors worldwide.
$6.95

CHARACTER DEVELOPMENT

EDUCATION FOR LIFE by J. Donald Walters. "A Revolutionary System of Education" is the appropriate sub-title of this book. The system described in the book is a catalyst for providing an education that includes the intellectual achievement plus interpersonal skills. In short, a well-rounded education. This book explains what to teach, how to teach it, when to teach it, and why. "His approach is innovative and his presentation effective. Parents, as well as educators, will be interested." —*Library Journal.* $9.95

THE HOME SCHOOL MANUAL (Third Edition) by Ted Wade. Mr. Wade and 17 other contributors tell you all about successful home education. Practical information you can put to work packed into 31 chapters and 9 appendices. Includes: reasons for home teaching; who shouldn't try home teaching; keeping it legal; being an effective teacher; when to begin; teaching specific subjects; finding materials and help; achieving quality. $15.50

ORDER FORM ON PAGE 128

HOME SCHOOLS: An Alternative
You do have a choice!
by Cheryl Gorder

BOOK REVIEWERS HAVE APPLAUDED THIS BOOK:

"Home Schools: An Alternative provides valuable encouragement for those parents who want to assume the responsibility for their children's education."
—HOME EDUCATION MAGAZINE

"This is one good little book. Author Cheryl Gorder coolly and logically presents what home schooling is, why people do it, and why we should be allowed to do it....Wonderful for convincing yourself or others that home schooling is OK."
—NEW BIG BOOK OF HOME LEARNING by Mary Pride

"The legal aspects are covered very well...Documented cases are cited and terminology explained for the benefit of parents who may come up against such in the future...The real meat, however, lies in Chapter 12. It alone, with its ideas, plans, addresses, learning materials, and other resources, would make this book invaluable to any parent undertaking the home education of their children....Find the thoroughly professional, motivating contents of the author."
—PARENTS & TEACHERS OF GIFTED CHILDREN

"How did something like home schooling metamorphose from a radical reaction against the establishment into a grassroots, mainstream movement? Cheryl Gorder's book is helping in untangling the threads of this metamorphosis. What makes a home schooling parent tick? Cheryl Gorder's book gives clear answers to these questions."
—THE LIGUORIAN

"This book is written to answer the many questions surrounding today's home-schooling movement in the United States. It is for a general audience and covers a variety of topics ranging from the religious and moral issues for home schools to the legal and educational issues raised by the movement."
—MARRIAGE & FAMILY LIVING

Additional reviews in *Booklist, Small Press Book Review, The Family Learning Connection, The South Dakota Magazine* & *Homesteaders News*.

THEY REACHED FOR THE STARS!

by Ruth Turk

DARE TO DREAM!
ANYBODY CAN BECOME A STAR!

Poor kids can become famous.
Unpopular kids can become actors.
Handicapped kids can find hidden talents.

These kids dared to dream:

- ☆ Michael Jackson
- ☆ Mary Lou Retton
- ☆ Michael J. Fox
- ☆ Oprah Winfrey
- ☆ Steven Spielberg
- ☆ Cyndi Lauper
- ☆ Dorothy Hamill
- ☆ Ray Charles
- ☆ Wilma Rudolph
- ☆ Ted Kennedy Jr.
- ☆ Dudley Moore
- ☆ Barbra Streisand

These people were once kids with disadvantages, but they dared to believe in themselves. They overcame great obstacles to become famous.

ISBN 0-933025-20-3 $11.95

The Sixth Sense

Practical Tips for Everyday Safety
By Joseph Niehaus

Safety Tips For:
✔ **Senior Citizens**
✔ **Students**
✔ **Employees**
✔ **Families**

These tips require:
No special training
No special background

"If there is just one book all citizens should read—this is the book."—James M. O'Dell, Chief of Police, Kettering, Ohio.

"I believe that this is an important book. I heartily recommend it."—Clyde S. Morgan, Police Captain, retired, Kettering, Ohio.

HOME BUSINESS

HOME BUSINESS RESOURCE GUIDE
by Cheryl Gorder

A guide to information to help start a home business and to find products for home businesses.

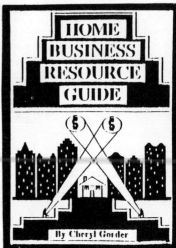

Includes:
Books for starting a home business
Courses for starting a home business
Wholesale products available to home businesses
Newsletters & magazines
Equipment and supplies use in home businesses

PLUS: DIRECTORY OF HOME BUSINESSES

SPECIAL FEATURE:
Profiles of successful home businesses

ISBN 0-933025-15-7   Price: $11.95

Did you know—
✓That there are over 7 million home businesses in the US?
✓That 1 in 7 American businesses is a home business?
✓That 20% of all American millionaires run a home business?
✓That 70% of all home businesses are run by women?

HOMELESSNESS

HOMELESS: WITHOUT ADDRESSES IN AMERICA by Cheryl Gorder

Blue Bird Publishing is pleased to announce a winner! The title Homeless: Without Addresses in America received a prestigious Benjamin Franklin award from the Publishers Marketing Association (PMA) during their annual banquet at the American Booksellers Association in Washington DC. The award announcements appear in the August 11, 1989 issue of Publishers Weekly.

ISBN 0-933025-11-4

$11.95

SIX MONTHS ON QUALITY BOOK'S "SMALL PRESS TOP 40".
Small Press Book Review—"Homeless is a model of design."
Sumner Dodge, Salvation Army—"Excellent book on the homeless."
Michael Dukakis—"Thanks for sharing your thoughts. Really appreciate it! Keep those ideas coming."
Millard Fuller, Habitat for Humanity—"God bless you for putting light on this disgraceful problem of homelessness in America."

THIS BOOK EXAMINES THE ENORMITY OF TODAY'S HOMELESSNESS, SHOWS WHO TODAY'S HOMELESS PEOPLE ARE AND WHAT IT'S LIKE TO BE HOMELESS, EXPLORES THE REASONS BEHIND HOMELESSNESS, AND LOOKS AT POSSIBLE SOLUTIONS.

ORDER FORM ON PAGE 128

ORDER FORM

To order more books from Blue Bird Publishing, use this handy order form.

_____ *Homeless! Without Addresses in America*	$11.95
_____ *Education for Life*	$9.95
_____ *Sharing Nature with Children*	$6.95
_____ *Home Schools: An Alternative* (3rd edition)	$11.95
_____ *Home Education Resource Guide* (revised)	$11.95
_____ *Spacedog's Best Friend*	$6.95
_____ *Home Business Resource Guide*	$11.95
_____ *Dr. Christman's Learn-to-Read Book*	$15.95
_____ *The Sixth Sense: Practical Tips for Everyday Safety*	$11.95
_____ *They Reached for the Stars!*	$11.95
_____ *Parents' Guide to Helping Kids Become "A" Students*	$11.95
Home School Manual	$15.50

Shipping Charges: $1.50 for first book. Add 50 cents for each additional book.

Total charges for books: _____

Total shipping charges: _____

TOTAL ENCLOSED: _____

NAME: _____

ADDRESS: _____

CITY, STATE, ZIP: _____

Telephone #: _____

Credit card orders call toll-free 1-800-654-1993

Purchase orders may be mailed or sent by FAX # (602) 983-7319. Wholesale and library orders given discount.

Send mail order to:

BLUE BIRD PUBLISHING
1713 East Broadway #306
Tempe AZ 85282
(602) 968-4088
FAX (602) 983-7319